EVIDENCE

IN

ATHENIAN COURTS

BY

ROBERT J. BONNER, PH.D.

ASSISTANT IN GREEK AND LATIN, UNIVERSITY OF CHICAGO

FORMERLY OF THE ONTARIO BAR

THE LAWBOOK EXCHANGE, LTD.

Clark, New Jersey

2006

ISBN-13: 978-1-58477-723-6
ISBN-10: 1-58477-723-0

Second printing 2008

The quality of this reprint is equivalent to the quality of the original work.

Printed in the United States of America on acid-free paper

THE LAWBOOK EXCHANGE, LTD.
33 Terminal Avenue
Clark, New Jersey 07066-1321

Please see our website for a selection of our other publications and fine facsimile reprints of classic works of legal history:
www.lawbookexchange.com

Library of Congress Cataloging-in-Publication Data

Bonner, Robert Johnson, 1868-1946.
Evidence in Athenian courts/ by Robert J. Bonner.
p. cm.
Includes bibliographical references and index.
ISBN-13: 978-1-58477-723-6 (alk. paper)
ISBN-10: 1-58477-723-0 (alk. paper)
1. Evidence (Greek law). Courts--Greece--Athens--History--To 1500. I. Title.
KL4350.B66 2006
347.38'506--dc22 2006010861

EVIDENCE

IN

ATHENIAN COURTS

BY

Robert J. Bonner, Ph.D.

ASSISTANT IN GREEK AND LATIN, UNIVERSITY OF CHICAGO
FORMERLY OF THE ONTARIO BAR

CHICAGO
THE UNIVERSITY OF CHICAGO PRESS
1905

PREFACE

No complete work on the subject of Evidence in Athenian courts has appeared since the admirable treatise of Meier and Schoemann, *Der attische Process*. Monographs, dissertations, and articles have been written on special points, such as oaths, slaves' evidence, perjury, and arbitrators; but these for the most part have been considered by Lipsius in his careful revision of Meier and Schoemann's work. Aristotle's *Constitution of Athens* has added something to our knowledge of the subject.[1] But neither the new material found in Aristotle nor that furnished by recently discovered epigraphical sources would be sufficient justification for a new discussion of a subject on which the labors of such competent scholars as Heffter, Platner, Meier, Schoemann, and Lipsius have been lavished. A few years ago, M. Beauchet,[2] while expressing admiration for *Der attische Process*, signified his intention of treating in a future work the subject of procedure, including evidence, and the constitution of the courts. Beauchet's reason for wishing to undertake the work appears to be his desire to round out his history of Athenian private law. And doubtless his method of treatment and his thorough knowledge of the science of law would enable him to do for these branches of Attic law what his own labors and those of Thonissen have already done for civil and criminal law.[3]

It was with no thought of attempting to anticipate M. Beauchet[4] that I undertook this work, for I doubt not that my point of view will be as fundamentally different from his as it is from that of the German writers on the subject. I have endeavored in the following pages to deal with the whole subject of evidence from the standpoint of English law, which, though it differs so widely at almost every point from the Athenian system, is yet admirably suited for the purpose, as it is the most perfectly rational system of rules ever devised for ascertaining the truth about matters in dispute. By the use of its divisions and categories I have been able to observe and classify considerable evidentiary matter in the speeches of the

[1] This material has, with one trifling exception (p. 44), already been noticed in its proper connection in these special treatises.

[2] Beauchet, *Histoire du droit privé des Athéniens* p. L.

[3] Cf. Dareste, *Nouvelles études d'histoire du droit*, pp. 58 f.

[4] It was not until I had almost completed my work that I became aware of M. Beauchet's intention.

Attic Orators which has been passed over in the purely philological works. I am well aware that many of the classifications employed were entirely unknown to the Athenian Orators, who concerned themselves but little about the real character of the evidence they produced. I need mention only Real and Expert Evidence, and the several subdivisions under Hearsay Evidence, as examples in point.

This plan has naturally involved the use of English legal terminology to translate the technical terms of Attic law—a practice which has the sanction of Charles R. Kennedy, a competent English lawyer, and of Dr. Sandys, an equally competent philologist. It is true that these equivalents are not always exact. Indeed, exact parallels are extremely rare. But the gain in vividness of conception seems to outweigh any possible loss of accuracy. A demurrer is not the same as a παραγραφή, but it occupies practically the same place in our legal system as παραγραφή occupied in the Athenian. And, in the same way, a prosecution for perjury differs as widely as possible from a δίκη ψευδομαρτυριῶν, but both are intended to achieve the same object, the prevention of false evidence. Frequent comparisons with the provisions of English law have been introduced for the purposes of illustration. It is hoped, too, that this feature will help the reader to appreciate more clearly both the excellencies and the shortcomings of the Athenian system.

The subject suggested itself in a course on the Attic Orators given by Professor Paul Shorey, head of the Greek Department of the University of Chicago; and throughout the preparation of the work I have constantly availed myself of his guidance and assistance, which, owing to his practical knowledge of Anglo-American law, have proved extremely valuable in ways too numerous to mention. To Professor Whittier, of the Law School of the University of Chicago, I am indebted for a number of suggestions. I wish to express my appreciation of the assistance rendered me by Professor Edward Capps, of the Greek Department of the University of Chicago. I subjoin a list of the books and monographs from which I have derived assistance. But to no single work do I owe so much as to Lipsius' revised edition of Meier and Schoemann's *Attische Process*, of which I have made constant use. And my debt has perhaps been greatest in those instances in which I have been unable to accept their conclusions.

R. J. BONNER.

THE UNIVERSITY OF CHICAGO,
April, 1905.

BOOKS AND ARTICLES CITED

BARRILLEAU, *Des sources du droit grec.* (Paris, 1883.)
BEAUCHET, *Histoire du droit privé de la République athénienne.* (Paris, 1897; 4 vols.)
BENTLEY, *Dissertations.* (Berlin, 1874.)
BLASS, *Die attische Beredsamkeit.* (Leipzig, 1887; 4 vols.)
BOECK, *Kleine Schriften.* (Leipzig, 1866; 7 books.)
BRÉHIER, *De Græcorum judiciorum origine.* (Paris, 1899.)
CAILLEMER, articles in Daremberg et Saglio, *Dictionnaire des antiquités grecques et romaines.* (Paris, 1873–96.)
DARESTE, *Nouvelles études d'histoire du droit.* (Paris, 1902.)
—— *Les plaidoyers civils de Demosthène.* (Paris, 1875; 2 vols.)
DITTENBERGER, "Antiphons' Tetralogien und das attische Criminalrecht," *Hermes*, Vol. XXXI, pp. 271 ff.; *ibid.*, Vol. XXXII, pp. 1 ff.
EGGER, "Si les Athéniens ont connu la profession d'avocat," *Mémoires de littérature ancienne* (Paris, 1862), pp. 355 ff.
GARLAND AND MCGEHEE, *English and American Encyclopædia of Law* (London, 1896.)
GILBERT, *Beiträge zur Entwickelungsgeschichte des griechischen Gerichtsverfahrens.* (Leipzig, 1896.)
GOODELL, "Aristotle on the Public Arbitrators," *American Journal of Philology*, Vol. XII, pp. 319 ff.
GREENIDGE, *The Legal Procedure of Cicero's Time.* (Oxford, 1901.)
GREENLEAF, *Evidence.* (16th Edition, Boston, 1899; 3 vols.)
GROTE, *History of Greece.* (12 vols.)
GUGGENHEIM, *Die Bedeutung der Folterung im attischen Recht.* (Zürich, 1882.)
HEADLAM, "Slave Torture in Attic Law," *Classical Review*, Vol. VII, pp. 1 ff.; *ibid.*, Vol. VIII, pp. 136 ff.
HEFFTER, *Die athenäische Gerichtsverfassung.* (Cologne, 1822.)
HERMANN, *De vestigiis institutorum veterum imprimis Atticorum, per Platonis de legibus libros indagandis.* (Marburg, 1836.)
HUBERT, *De arbitris Atticis et privatis et publicis.* (Leipzig, 1885.)
JEBB, *The Attic Orators.* (London, 1893; 2 vols.)
KENNEDY, *Demosthenes.* (Bohn's Series; 5 vols.)
—— Articles in SMITH'S *Dictionary of Greek and Roman Antiquities.* (London, 1890.)
KÖHLER, "Attische Inschriften," *Hermes*, 1867, p. 27.
LIPSIUS, "Ueber das neugefundene Buch des Aristotles vom Staat Athener," *Bericht der Königlichen Sächsischen Gesellschaft der Wissenschaften*, 1891, pp. 41 ff.
MAHAFFY, *Social Life in Greece.* (London, 1894.)
MAINE, *Ancient Law.*
MEDERLE, *De jurisjurandi in lite Attica decem oratorum aetate usu.* (Munich, 1902.)
MEIER AND SCHOEMANN, *Der attische Process;* revised by LIPSIUS. (Berlin, 1883–77; 2 vols.; cited as M. S. L.)
MEUSS, *De "ἀπαγωγῆς" actione apud Athenienses.* (Warsaw, 1884.)
MOY, *Étude sur les plaidoyers d'Isée.* (Paris, 1876.)

PHILIPPI, *Der Areopag und die Epheten.* (Berlin, 1874.)

PLATNER, *Der Process und die Klagen bei den Attikern.* (Darmstadt, 1824–25.)

POLLOCK, *Torts* (Webb's edition, St. Louis, 1894.)

POLLOCK AND MAITLAND, *History of English Law.* (Boston, 1899; 2 vols.)

RENTZSCH, *De Δίκη ψευδομαρτυριῶν in jure Attico.* (Leipzig, 1901.)

ROHDE, *Psyche.* (Freiburg, 1890; 2 vols.)

SANDYS, *Aristotle's Constitution of Athens.* (London, 1893.)

SANDYS AND PALEY, *Select Private Orations of Demosthenes.* (Cambridge, 1896; 2 vols.)

SIMON, "Zur griechischen Alterthümern," *Wiener Studien*, Vol. XII, p. 70.

SOROF, "Die ἀπαγωγή in Mörderprocessen," *Neues Jahrbuch für Philologie*, Vol. CXXVII, No. 2, pp. 105 ff.

STEPHENS, *A Digest of the Law of Evidence.* (New York, 1898.)

TELFY, *Corpus juris attici.* (1868.)

THALHEIM, articles in Pauly-Wissowa, *Real-Encyclopädia.* (Stuttgart, 1896.)

THAYER, *A Preliminary Treatise on Evidence at the Common Law.* (Boston, 1898.)

THOMPSON, "Slave Torture in Athens," *Classical Review*, Vol. VIII, p. 136.

THONISSEN, *Le droit pênal de la République athénienne.* (Brussels, 1875.)

VOLKMANN, *Die Rhetorik der Griechen und Römer.* (Leipzig, 1882.)

WASZYNSKI, *De servis Atheniensium publicis.* (Berlin, 1898.)

WIGMORE, *Evidence in Trials at Common Law.* (Boston, 1904; 4 vols.)

WILAMOWITZ, *Die erste Rede des Antiphons.*

ZIEBARTH, *De jurejurando in jure Graeco quaestiones.* (Göttingen, 1892.)

TABLE OF CONTENTS

CHAPTER I

INTRODUCTION

The experience of Athens has shown that law may be administered satisfactorily without a professional class either of judges or of lawyers. Magistrates chosen by lot were constantly required to exercise important judicial functions for which they had no special training; nor were they able to gain a fund of knowledge by experience, as they held office for one year only. In all probability, the general efficiency of the magistrates was largely due to the practice which permitted them to choose their own assessors. This enabled a weak magistrate to secure the assistance of a competent man to aid him in his official duties. There is, however, no indication that these assessors were reappointed by succeeding magistrates, as is the case in the British system of government, where deputies may continue to hold office under different ministers of the crown.

With the object of making each citizen take his full share in public life, and of preserving equality (ἰσοτιμία) in the citizen body, litigants, if citizens, were required to take their own cases in court. But this was an ideal beyond the possibility of achievement even in the Athens of Pericles. And so there arose a class of men whose business it was to write speeches for those who were unequal to the task of pleading their own cases. These **λογογράφοι** did to a certain degree constitute a professional class, but they were not lawyers in our sense of the word. A knowledge of rhetoric was quite as important for their success as a knowledge of law. Moreover, the necessity of fitting the speech to the character of his client tended to keep the speech-writer in the background. Indeed, every artifice was resorted to in order to keep up the delusion that the litigant had prepared his own speech.

Perhaps a nearer parallel to the modern lawyer is found in the advocate (συνήγορος), who was permitted to address the jury on behalf of a litigant. The fourth oration of Isæus, which is said to have been delivered by himself as an advocate, is extremely effective and strikingly similar in some respects to the address of a modern counsel; and indications are not wanting that certain individuals did make it a practice to render services of this kind in a professional way. The excuses, based on friendship to one party or hostility to the other, that are offered as a reason for appearing before the court as an advocate were in many cases designed to veil the professional character of the service; and the very fact that remuneration was forbidden by law is a tacit recognition of the natural tendency of these services to become professional. Another avenue to professionalism was closed by the law which prevented a man's being selected more than once as public advocate to defend a law before the Thesmothetæ.[1] The ἐξηγηταί, who expounded the traditional rules and forms concerning religious observances, resemble the priest rather than the jurist. The speech-writer in the course of his experience no doubt acquired a considerable fund of legal knowledge. But the conditions of his art forbade a display of an intimate knowledge of law, which would not be in keeping with the character of his client as a layman.[2] This applies particularly to matters of practice and procedure. When technicalities were relied upon, they were always accompanied by a full discussion of the facts of the case. Opponents were ever ready to appeal to the jury's suspicion of all pleas that to the lay mind seemed to be evasions. Nothing was so prejudicial to a litigant's chances of success as an unwillingness to rest his case on its merits.[3] The natural result of this was to subordinate law to fact. Hence pleading remained simple. The tendency toward intricacy, so well known in all modern systems, was effectually checked. Under these circumstances, the rules of evidence are comparatively few in number and simple in form. Elaborate exceptions and fine distinctions are entirely wanting.

Our materials for constructing the history of the law of evidence are comparatively limited. The evidentiary oath constitutes the sole exception, for its history can be traced with considerable certainty. But even here there are serious gaps. We are at a loss to know how the evidentiary oath degenerated into the formal and almost meaningless party oath sworn by both parties to a suit when the pleadings were filed, or how it came to be extended to witnesses.[4] But the reason for the provision requiring evidence to be written, the origin of arbitration, and the nature of the original jurisdiction of magistrates which survived in the ἀνάκρισις present questions that can be answered only by conjecture. And there are many other cases where the practice of the Orators can be thoroughly understood only in the light of history, which unfortunately we are not able to reconstruct.

The object of all rules of evidence is to secure the best evidence. Herein lies the weakness of the Athenian system of popular courts, which determined questions both of law and of fact. For example, the provisions for the exclusion of irrelevant matter are very inadequate, and the superiority

[1] D. 20:152.

[2] D. 54:17, with Sandys' note.

[3] D. 35:2; 37:21; 44:57; Isæ. 7:3.

[4] Cf. p. 75.

of documentary evidence over parole evidence, or of originals over copies, was never fully appreciated. Without a judge, questions of practice and procedure could not be decided apart from questions of fact; and rules of evidence could not be adequately enforced, nor could improper evidence be effectually excluded. The only course open to a pleader was to raise objections in court, in the hope that the jury in reaching a decision might be prejudiced against the other side; or the party who introduced improper evidence could in certain cases be prosecuted by a *δίκη ψευδομαρτυριῶν*. Arbitrators may very well have been empowered to determine questions regarding the admissibility of evidence and the competency of witnesses, but there are no instances of the exercise of such powers. The Areopagus was better provided with machinery for securing obedience to its rules than were the Heliastic courts, but, in comparison with the provisions of modern legal systems, it seems to have been far from adequate.

The Orators frequently address the jury as if they were addressing the whole Athenian people; and, indeed, the law courts are conceived of as being, along with the assembly, a medium through which the sovereign people expressed its will. The judicial functions which the assembly assumed in case of *εἰσαγγελία*, *μήνυσις*, and *προβολή* helped to obscure the distinction between a judicial and a deliberative body. This political character of the jury encouraged speakers to resort to the methods of the assembly. Hence we find appeals to the gratitude of the jury for the public services of a litigant or his ancestors. The financial benefits that would accrue to the state are also dwelt upon, in perfect confidence that the selfishness of the citizens would prove a shield against any possible objections from an opponent. Appeals to prejudices of all sorts find a readier response in a large body than in a small, where the sense of responsibility is greater than where it is shared with a numerous body. The almost invariable plea of litigants for a fair hearing is suggestive of a political meeting rather than of a judicial body; and the fate of Apollodorus, to whom a jury refused to listen at all, shows that it was not an unnecessary plea.[1] The speech-writer, in the character of a layman pleading his case as best he could, did not feel his responsibility to the same extent as he would had he appeared in person, nor was due weight given by the jury to his opinions as to the meaning and application of the law.

The practice of deciding each case on its merits, according to the whims and prejudices of the moment, without regard to precedents, deprives us of an important source of information. The citation of cases would not only largely increase our materials, but would give us an insight into the

[1] D. 45:6.

history of the various rules. Only on rare occasions do we know how a case was decided; and even then the knowledge is of little or no assistance, as there is no indication of the reasons for the decisions. Even the speeches of the Orators, which constitute by far the most important sources of information, are often mere *ex parte* statements. In matters of law they are, on the whole, reliable, but in not a few instances a different complexion was perhaps given to a rule by the reply of an opponent. For example, it would be very helpful to know why Aphobus gave evidence against his uncle, or what Bœotus said in answer to the contention of Mantitheus that Crito by reason of his interest in the case was not a competent witness.[1]

Owing to the entire subordination of legal to rhetorical training, legal education was never developed to any great extent. Such exercises as Antiphon's tetralogies were never as important or as popular at Athens as were the *controversiae* at Rome. The meager treatment of law in works on rhetoric falls far short of a science of law. Plato's work came too late materially to influence lawmaking and the scientific study of law. The *responsa* of the Roman jurisconsults show us what Athenian jurists might under different circumstances have done for Attic law.

CHAPTER II

IRRELEVANT EVIDENCE

Following the practice of the Orators, I use the term "irrelevant" to include everything that does not bear directly upon the issue.[2] This is the meaning which laymen usually attach to the word. As to the meaning of the term in English legal phraseology, several different theories have been advanced;[3] but the niceties and refinements of these discussions are entirely foreign to Attic law, which simply forbade the introduction of evidence that did not bear on the case.

There are in the speeches of the Orators a number of protests against the prevailing practice[4] of introducing irrelevant matters into the discussion of a case. Sometimes it is urged that it is impossible within the time

[1] Cf. pp. 45, 28.

[2] Such expressions as *εἰς τὸ πρᾶγμα, πρὸς τὰ κατηγορημένα, περὶ τοῦ πράγματος, εἰς αὐτὸν τὸν φόνον*, are used to characterize relevant evidence, while irrelevant evidence is that which is *ἔξω τοῦ πράγματος, ἔξω τῆς κατηγορίας, ἔξω τῆς γραφῆς*.

[3] Sir James Stephens, *A Digest of the Law of Evidence*, Introduction, p. xvi; Thayer, pp. 263 ff.; Wigmore, § 12.

[4] Cf. Lys. 12:38.

allowed to discuss adequately the main issue, if one's attention is distracted by all sorts of irrelevant charges.[1] At other times it is said that irrelevant charges and excuses are the resort of those who are unable to prove their cases. They hope thus to divert the mind of the jurors from the real issue,[2] though jurors who were influenced by anything that did not bear directly on the matter in hand could not be free from blame.[3] Moreover, the success of those who relied on winning their cases by arguments and evidence which were not pertinent to the case before the court could not fail to encourage sycophants.[4] These objections have reference to the speeches rather than to the evidence; but they undoubtedly were intended to include the depositions which corroborated the speeches. In this respect the rule against irrelevancy differed from the hearsay rule, which applied to evidence alone. The chief check upon the introduction of extraneous and irrelevant matter before the court applied only to the Areopagus.[5] Here the prosecutor had to take an especially solemn oath to confine himself to the charge on the record. The witnesses, too, were obliged to swear to the guilt or innocence of the accused.[6]

The language of Pollux includes both prosecutor and defendant in restrictions upon the nature of the speeches before the Areopagus. It was the purpose of these restrictions to confine the parties closely to the charge;[7] and Philippi is unquestionably right in concluding that the defendant took the same oath as the prosecutor.[8] There are some indications that these restrictions were attended with a certain degree of success, for the defendant in the Herodes murder trial maintained that his accusers chose to indict him as an evildoer (κακοῦργος) rather than as a murderer, because they were well aware that no witness would appear against him if the solemn oath were required.[9] The danger of prejudicing his case with the jury would naturally make a man cautious about going beyond the charge on the record; and we find a defendant before the Areopagus not only expressing confidence that the jurors will not allow themselves to be misled by attacks on his record as a citizen, but actually refraining from answering them.[10] And, further, it is significant of the temper of the Areopagus in this connection to find extraneous matters introduced with

[1] D. 41:13; 45:47. [2] D. 58:23; 59:5.

[3] Ant. 6:10. Cf. the juror's oath in D. 24:150 which bound him to vote only on the matter at issue.

[4] Lyc. 1:13. [5] Cf. Arist., *Rhet.*, 1, 1:5 ff.; Lucian, *Anacharsis*, 19.

[6] Ant. 6:9; 5:11 ff.; cf. Jebb, Vol. I, p. 26.

[7] Pollux 8:117. [8] Philippi, p. 90. [9] Ant. 5:15.

[10] Ant. 6:9 ff.; Blass, Vol. I, p. 199.

an apology.[1] But at a later period Lycurgus, after reminding the Areopagus of the respect and esteem which the court enjoyed, insists that they ought not to allow the introduction of matter not pertinent to the issue.[2]

The means that the Areopagus, in common with other courts, had at its disposal for enforcing obedience were clumsy and inadequate when compared with the machinery of a modern court presided over by a judge charged with the duty of enforcing rules of procedure. Apart from its power to give an adverse verdict, a jury could and did freely express its disapproval of the argument used by a speaker, or bade him stick to the main issue.[3] In case a speaker before the Areopagus introduced extraneous matter, he was promptly silenced by the herald.[4] In other courts, too, except in cases of δοκιμασία, it was well understood that speeches and evidence ought to be relevant,[5] and complaints against speakers who do not confine themselves to the issue are common.[6] In view of the extreme frequency of irrelevant evidence, one wonders that protests are not more common; but the apologies that sometimes usher in or conclude digressions are indications that the rule could not be disregarded with impunity.[7]

It is reasonable to suppose, however, that there were some virtual exceptions to the rule, even though no express mention of them is made. On no other supposition can we account for the amount of extraneous matter found in the speeches of the Orators. A practice that calls forth no objections cannot be altogether irregular.

In criminal cases we find constant endeavors to prove that the defendant had on previous occasions either committed or attempted to commit a similar crime. Probably the most striking instance of this occurs in the trial of a woman charged with poisoning her husband. These are the facts of the case, in brief: The favorite slave of one Philoneus had administered what she supposed to be a love-potion to her master and a friend who was dining with him. The drug was a poison, and both men succumbed to its effects. The son of the friend of Philoneus, on reaching his majority, accused his stepmother of the crime. He claimed that she had induced the girl to administer to the two men what she thought was a harmless philter. His father, according to his dying declaration, had on several occasions caught the accused in the act of administering drugs to him. As corroboration of the statement of the deceased, the plaintiff challenged the production of slaves who, he claimed, knew of these attempts.

1 Lys. 3:44.

2 Lyc. 1:13.

3 Ant. 5:90; 6:8 ff.; D. 57:66; Hyper. 3:10, 31; Isæ. 6:62.

4 Lucian, *Anachar.*, 19.

5 Lys. 16:9.

6 Lys. 9:1 ff.; 12:36.

7 D. 29:50; 38:26; 57:59, 63.

Without such evidence it was hopeless to try to connect the woman with the crime.[1] On the plea of telling the whole story, the plaintiff in Ariston v. Conon, a case of assault and battery in which Conon's sons were the real offenders, produces evidence to prove that two years before he had been assaulted, though not seriously, by the sons alone.[2] This was important, as it must have gone a long way to disprove the claim of Conon that it was a trifling affair, such as young men about town often engaged in as a result of disputes arising out of *affaires de cœur*.[3] The previous assault shows the animus at the bottom of the second. If evidence of the first were excluded, the real character of the second would be difficult to establish. Apollodorus, in a civil suit against Polycles for failure to relieve him of his trierarchy at the time appointed, proves by witnesses a similar failure of the defendant to relieve Euripides.[4]

The vital importance in criminal matters of establishing a motive for the crime was clearly recognized by prosecutors, and often led to the introduction of matter that was apparently irrelevant. An attempt was made to establish a motive for the murder of Herodes by alleging that the crime was committed as a favor to Lucinus. It was claimed that a letter was found, which announced the murder to Lucinus. The prosecution evidently attempted to show, also, that Lucinus had an interest in the death of Herodes. And the defendant, without protest on his part, undertook the task of explaining that Lucinus had no possible reason for desiring the death of Herodes.[5] On the other hand, it might often be necessary to introduce evidence which, strictly speaking, had nothing to do with the issue on hand, in order to show that there was no motive for the crime. A case in Lysias, involving the charge of wounding with intent, shows the unfairness of the rule requiring witnesses to swear to the truth or falsity of the charge. The defendant desired quite properly to show that there was no malice aforethought. To do this it was desirable to establish a certain fact, which bore no direct relation to the assault, and as it turned out to be impossible to procure witnesses who were aware both of the assault and of the fact in question, he was unable to prove the point.[6]

It was the common practice, on the trial of a special plea (παραγραφή), to go over the entire case and introduce all the evidence,[7] for it was well known that jurors always looked to the main issue as well as to the special plea.[8] Indeed, the only reason for raising a special plea, if we may trust

[1] Ant. 1:9, 14 ff., 29. English practice allows proof of previous attempts to establish malice or intent.

[2] D. 54:3 ff.

[3] D. 54:14.

[4] D. 50:68; cf. 21:23.

[5] Ant. 5:53, 60.

[6] Lys. 4:2 ff.

[7] D. 36:3.

[8] D. 45:51.

the opinion of a discomfited litigant,[1] was the advantage of having the first speech. It was customary, too, in prosecutions for perjury to bring forward again the main issue in the original case.[2] But the practice is not unchallenged. The objection of the plaintiff in Apollodorus v. Stephanus, however, comes with poor grace from a man who himself toward the end of the same speech indulges in a fierce tirade against Phormio, who was not a party to the suit.[3] Demosthenes, in his speech in behalf of Phanus, who was prosecuted by Aphobus for false evidence in Demosthenes v. Aphobus, apologizes for a long digression in which he discusses the main issue of the original suit. The apology, however, does not imply a recognition of the impropriety of introducing irrelevant matter, but is rather intended to anticipate any criticism for his apparent neglect of the interests of his client, who was in grave danger.[4]

Another instance of what is apparently irrelevant evidence is testimony to show that the speaker is not a sycophant; for the Athenian prejudice against these professional litigants made it highly desirable to avoid any suspicion on that score.[5] This might be done by proof that the speaker was not litigious,[6] or that he had made an effort to settle the case amicably, or that he had good cause for hostility against his opponent and was prompted to take action against him by a desire for revenge.[7] On the other hand, it was to a speaker's interest to expose his opponent to the odium attaching to sycophancy, or to lay bare his corrupt or ulterior motive for bringing the suit.[8] The plaintiff in Apollodorus v. Phormio claims that no evidence is more to the point than proof that his opponent is a sycophant.[9]

What may conveniently be designated character evidence will be found to include the bulk of the remaining cases of irrelevant evidence.[10] Allegations regarding character are found in some cases even before the Areopagus.[11] In others they are conspicuously absent.[12] The recital of the services of a man or of his ancestors is especially frequent. Antiphon has put the objection to these recitals rather effectively: "Neither should a man's good deeds save him from condemnation if guilty, nor his evil deeds, apart from the charge against him, condemn him if innocent."[13] But when once

[1] D. 45:6. [2] D. 29:9, 27 ff. [3] D. 45:47 ff., 71.

[4] D. 29:50; cf. Isæ. 5:5. Suit for performance of suretyship introduces the whole matter.

[5] Arist., *Acharn.*, 559, 818 ff.; Ant. 5:80.

[6] D. 48:3. [7] D. 21:77; 59:1 ff. [8] Ant. 6:36. [9] D. 36:54.

[10] Arist., *Rhet.*, 1:15, 18: *καὶ αἱ μὲν* [*μαρτυρίαι*] *περὶ τοῦ πράγματος αἱ δὲ περὶ τοῦ ἤθους.*

[11] Lys. 3:47; 7:31. [12] Ant. 6; Lys. 4. [13] Ant. 5:11.

a man was allowed freely to parade his own and his ancestors' public services, it was an easy step to the conclusion of Lysias that, if the jury listened to a recital of a man's good deeds, his opponents ought to be allowed to prove his evil deeds.[1] This is precisely the ground upon which alone English law permits a prosecutor to show that the accused does not bear a good reputation among his neighbors; but character evidence in this sense has, generally speaking, no place in English civil suits. Aristotle distinguishes character evidence from other evidence. If regular evidence fails a litigant, he can always bring testimony regarding his own and his adversary's character.[2] It was not considered bad taste to descend to vulgar personalities. Demosthenes' abuse of Æschines or Meidias will at once occur to every reader in this connection. A man's moral failings, his disposition, and his physical peculiarities were made the subject of ridicule and invective. The speeches in the suits between Apollodorus and Phormio show both parties indulging in personalities.[3] Nor did a man's relatives escape.[4] The Greeks were peculiarly sensitive to physical defects or improper conduct in public; and speakers occasionally work on this prejudice.[5] The injustice of such a prejudice is well voiced by Lysias.[6]

It was not felt by the Greeks that supernatural signs, omens, portents, and oracles were irrelevant. These things were regarded as the judgments of heaven and were respected as such. A somewhat similar feeling underlay the trial by "ordeal," which in old English law was an appeal to *judicium dei*. Antiphon justifies the introduction of evidence relating to omens by referring to the attention given them by those in charge of the public affairs. Then evidence is produced to show that the fellow-voyagers of the defendant always enjoyed most favorable weather, and his presence never affected sacrifices unfavorably.[7] Andocides' opponents attempt to anticipate evidence of this kind by saying that the gods preserved him through all his dangers that he might perish at the hands of his accusers in Athens.[8] Demosthenes, too, quotes an oracle to show that Meidias in injuring a choregus was guilty of impiety;[9] and Aristotle discusses and

[1] Lys. 14:24.

[2] Arist., *Rhet.*, 1:15, 18.

[3] D. 36:51 ff.; 45:71 ff.

[4] Lys. 13:67 ff.

[5] D. 37:52; 45:68 ff., and Sandys' note.

[6] *ὥστε οὐκ ἄξιον ἀπ' ὄψεως, ὦ βουλή, οὔτε φιλεῖν οὔτε μισεῖν οὐδένα, ἀλλ' ἐκ τῶν ἔργων σκοπεῖν. πολλοὶ μὲν γὰρ μικρὸν διαλεγόμενοι καὶ κοσμίως περιερχόμενοι μεγάλων κακῶν αἴτιοι γεγόνασιν, ἕτεροι δὲ τῶν τοιούτων ἀμελοῦντες πολλὰ κἀγαθὰ ὑμᾶς εἰσιν εἰργασμένοι.* Lys. 16:19.

[7] Ant. 5:81 ff.

[8] And. 1:137.

[9] D. 21:51 ff.; cf. 43:66.

recommends the use of proverbs as evidence.[1] A curious instance of the use of dreams as evidence occurs in Polyeuctus v. Euxenippus. A piece of land, which was the subject of a dispute between two tribes, was said to be sacred to Amphiaraus. Three men were ordered by the assembly to sleep in the temple of the divinity to see if their dreams would throw light on the matter.[2]

CHAPTER III

HEARSAY EVIDENCE

Hearsay evidence (ἀκοὴν μαρτυρεῖν) was expressly forbidden by law, on the ground of the general untrustworthiness of reported statements as compared with the evidence of eyewitnesses.[3] The chief reason for the modern prohibition of hearsay evidence is the impossibility of testing the credibility of the original witness and of ascertaining "what were his powers of perception, his opportunities for observation, his attentiveness in observing, the strength of his recollection, and his disposition to speak the truth."[4]

As cross-examination of witnesses was unknown in Athenian courts, the objections to hearsay evidence did not assume as definite a shape as they do in the language of a modern lawyer. The means of excluding hearsay evidence were comparatively meager. The witness who deceived the court by giving hearsay as original evidence was liable to prosecution for perjury, and the party in whose interest he appeared was also liable to an action for suborning illegal evidence.[5] There is no indication that an arbitrator ever excluded such evidence. Andocides tells of an irregular accusation made against him in a special meeting of the senate to hear the King Archon's report regarding the initiation of candidates in the Eleusinian Mysteries, which failed because it was supported only by hearsay evidence.[6] When improper evidence was once produced in court, the only means of attacking it was to make a vigorous objection in the hope of prejudicing the jury against the whole case.[7]

A general exception to the rule was recognized in the case of the death of the original witness. The scope of this exception will be indicated more clearly by a classification of the various cases that are included therein.

[1] Arist., *Rhet.*, 1:15, 14.

[2] Hyper. 3:14 ff.

[3] Isæ. 6:53; D. 57:4. This prohibition applies to a διαμαρτυρία; D. 44:55.

[4] Greenleaf, *Evidence*, Vol. I, §98.

[5] Cf. p. 93.

[6] And. 1:110 f.

[7] D. 44:55; 46:7; 57:4.

ANTE-MORTEM STATEMENTS OR DYING DECLARATIONS

If a man had, through violence or plots, been brought to the point of death, he might, by taking certain precautions, insure the punishment of his murderer in case death ensued. He might summon his relatives and friends and tell them who was responsible for his death. A solemn injunction to punish the criminal was always added. Or he might, in the absence of friends or relatives, commit his statement to writing and intrust it to his slaves, to enable them as informers to prosecute the murderer.[1] In English law dying declarations are limited to homicide cases.

At least three recorded cases of ante-mortem statements are found in the Orators. The case against the stepmother in Antiphon depended entirely upon a dying declaration of the deceased made in presence of his son, who afterward prosecuted his stepmother for procuring his father's death by poison. As the son was the prosecutor, he could not give evidence of his father's communication. Accordingly, the story of the murder was incorporated in the speech and corroborated to a certain extent by the defendant's refusal to give up her slaves for examination by torture. It was claimed that these slaves were aware of her designs upon her husband's life.

Where several relatives were cognizant of a dying declaration, one could act as prosecutor and the rest appear as witnesses, as in the prosecution of Agoratus, who, as an informer under the Thirty, had been the means of putting to death a number of leading democrats. Upon the restoration of democracy he was charged with the death of Dionysodorus. At the trial some of his relatives testified that on the eve of his execution he charged Agoratus[2] with responsibility for his death.

There is no instance of a written declaration being intrusted to slaves. Guggenheim is doubtless correct in regarding the slaves in such cases as informers rather than as witnesses.[3] An incident in one of Antiphon's hypothetical tetralogies may be noted here.[4] The only evidence against the accused is the statement of a dying slave who recognized him as the assailant of his master and himself. He had been in attendance on his master at a late supper. On their return home they had been murderously assaulted. The master was killed and the slave mortally wounded. It was maintained that the slave, on being questioned by some men who

[1] Ant. 1:29, 30; cf. Guggenheim, p. 7.

[2] Lys. 13:41.

[3] Guggenheim, p. 7; cf. Philippi, *Der Areopag*, p. 81.

[4] Ant. A. α. 9. Dittenberger (*Hermes*, Vol. XXXI, p. 271; Vol. XXXII, p. 1) has shown that no reliance is to be placed on the tetralogies in regard to questions of law.

found him in a dying state, had positively identified the murderer. Guggenheim treats this slave as an informer, though he admits that all the characteristics of an information are lacking. He mentions the δοκιμασία, or inquiry into the truth of the information and the ἄδεια, or immunity from punishment; and he might have added that the informer did not appear before any magistrate or official body to lay his information.[1] But a comparison with the practice in the case of dying declarations shows that, just as the death of the witness renders it necessary to dispense with the usual formalities and safeguards, so the death of a slave permits the omission of the usual formalities and safeguards connected with an information. The importance attached by the Athenians to dying injunctions is shown by the fact that forgiveness by the deceased of an accidental mortal injury is a bar to prosecution for homicide.[2]

DECLARATIONS ABOUT PEDIGREE OR MATTERS RELATING TO FAMILY HISTORY

Another important exception to the hearsay rule, which prevails both in English and in Athenian practice, occurs in the case of declarations about pedigree or matters of family history.[3] Pedigree includes birth, marriage, and death, as well as relationship and descent. One of Demosthenes' cases contains several illustrations. In a contest for the property of Hagnias, who died intestate, it was vital to the claim of the plaintiff to prove that Phylomache, his great-grandmother, was full sister to Polemo, father of Hagnias the intestate, and that Polemo was an only son.[4] Members of the deme to which Polemo belonged testified that they had never before heard that he had a brother, and that Phylomache was reputed to be his full sister. He next produced the great-grandsons of a cousin of Polemo, who testified to a declaration of their father to the same effect.[5]

The strict English rule admits only the declarations of deceased persons who were related to the person in question by blood or marriage. In some jurisdictions the rule is extended to include others who were intimately connected with the person.[6] In like manner, the Athenian court admitted the declarations of members of the same deme, who were naturally closely associated with each other.[7] Another witness in the case cited

[1] Guggenheim, pp. 8 f. δοκιμασία is rather loosely used of a purely informal inquiry which has little or nothing in common with the regular δοκιμασία.

[2] D. 38:59; Plato, *Republic*, 451 B; Euripides, *Hipp.*, 1449.

[3] Wigmore, *Evidence*, § 1503; cf. Plato, *Timæus*, 40 E; Isæ. 8:6.

[4] D. 43:38, 39.

[5] D. 43:35 f.

[6] Relations by marriage included only husband and wife (Wigmore, § 1486).

[7] D. 43:35.

above reports the declaration of a female relative of Polemo.[1] Thus the declaration of one who would not himself be a competent witness might be evidenced in court.[2]

The English courts have admitted inscriptions on tombstones and other funeral monuments as a species of hearsay evidence. The presumption is that the relatives of the family would not permit a record of this kind, if it were not true.[3] This was also the Athenian practice. Evidence was offered in one case to show that there was a black urn on the tomb of the person whose property was in dispute. The purpose of the evidence was to show that the deceased was unmarried.[4] Here belongs evidence of relationship drawn from the possession of a common burial ground.[5] The philosophy of it appears in a question of the plaintiff in Euxitheus v. Eubulides: *καίτοι τίς ἐστιν ὅστις ἂν εἰς τὰ πατρῷα μνήματα τοὺς μηδὲν ἐν γένει τιθέναι εἴασεν;*[6] Marriages of ancestors were proved by declarations of deceased relatives;[7] but where the witnesses who were present at a marriage are available they were produced.[8] They are usually the relatives of the contracting parties.[9] Family conduct may amount to a tacit recognition of relationship. If a father treats a boy as his legitimate son, this amounts to a daily assertion that he is a legitimate son; and evidence to this effect is really hearsay evidence.[10] A good instance of proof of this kind is furnished by Isæus,[11] who actually treats it as hearsay evidence.

ENTRIES IN ACCOUNT-BOOKS

Under the head of written hearsay evidence in English law come entries made in books in the course of business. The most common instances in the Orators are the books and papers of deceased bankers. Apollodorus is said to have collected large sums of money from his father's debtors by using the banker's accounts as evidence.[12] The Athenian custom of making an exception in case of bankers' contracts, and dispensing with the usual witnesses, made it necessary to rely on the books.[13] In the case of ordinary debts, either account-books containing a memorandum of the

[1] D. 43:37, 46.

[2] This is contrary to English practice (Wigmore, § 1510).

[3] Vowels v. Young, 13, Vesey, p. 144.

[4] D. 44:18, 30.

[5] D. 43:79, 80.

[6] D. 57:28.

[7] D. 43:44, 45.

[8] D. 57:41, 43.

[9] Isæ. 8:14.

[10] 4 Campbell, 416; cf. Wigmore, § 1495.

[11] Isæ. 8:14–18. Cf. Isæ. 3:77. Cf. infra p. 27.

[12] D. 36:20; cf. D. 52:6, where the same Apollodorus used his father's books to resist a claim.

[13] Isoc. 17:2.

debt are put in evidence, or the testimony of persons who heard the deceased say that certain moneys were owing him. The English rules would not admit this testimony, as it is neither a dying declaration nor the record of a business transaction. In a case in which the plaintiff sought to recover sums of money that were owing to one Polyeuctus and his wife, the debt to Polyeuctus was proved by a witness who heard him speak of the matter on his death-bed, while the wife on her death-bed left a written statement. This document was put in without the evidence of the witnesses in whose presence it was drawn up.[1] Such a document, as it was not prepared in the course of business, would not be admitted in an English court.

STATEMENTS OF POETS AND OTHER ILLUSTRIOUS MEN

Aristotle says that the opinions of poets and other distinguished men may be used as testimony. He mentions, among others, the case of Solon, who is said to have supported the claim of Athens to the island of Salamis against Megara by reciting a couplet from Homer.[2] None of the cases referred to are judicial trials, but there is no doubt that such evidence was admissible in the courts. English law permits the use of historical works to prove facts of a public and general nature, if not recent.

ADMISSIONS OF PARTIES AND OTHERS

Up to this point the various exceptions considered all come under the rule that permitted hearsay evidence when the original witness was dead. But we find a class of cases in which hearsay evidence was admitted without protest, though the original witness was not dead. The reason for the exception was the impossibility of producing the witness in court, either because of his incompetency, or because of his unwillingness to testify. There is no indication that the Orators recognized evidence of this character as hearsay. Parties to a suit were not competent to be regular witnesses. It is true that a litigant could question his opponent in court or at any preliminary hearing of the case; but in court at least a speaker rarely availed himself of this privilege.[3] He preferred, if possible, to produce a witness in whose presence the other side had made damaging admissions, either voluntarily or in answer to questions.[4] This corresponds with English practice, which permits evidence of such admissions to be produced.

In addition to these, we have several instances of the production of evidence of admissions and statements made by persons who are not parties to the suit. Thus in one case the admissions of a woman were allowed

[1] D. 41:9, 10.

[2] Arist., *Rhet.*, I, 15, 13; cf. Quint., V, 11, 39, 40.

[3] Cf. p. 57.

[4] D. 30:19, 20; 50:26; 58:33; Lys. 32:9.

to be brought out in evidence. As the litigation was connected with her father's estate, she was virtually, if not technically, a party to the suit.[1]

There are also admissions of persons who were so closely associated with the parties as to be practically in league with them. These may be conveniently classed as the admissions or statements of persons who for some reason or other refused to give evidence. Sometimes they were witnesses for the other side. An instance occurs in Isæus, where the admission of one Hierocles is introduced. He was, it is alleged, in collusion with the defendant in producing a forged will.[2] Chrysippus v. Phormio furnishes another example. Lampis, the agent of Phormio, at first denied to the plaintiff that he had received a certain sum of money; but later, being tampered with by Phormio, he virtually became his witness against the plaintiff, who then produced evidence of his denial of the receipt of the money.[3]

Another instance of hearsay evidence involves both the admissions of an opponent and the unwillingness of witnesses to testify. Lysias asserts that Eratosthenes, whom he charged with the murder of his brother, was one of the five ephors at Athens who constituted a revolutionary committee appointed by the oligarchic clubs to pave the way for the establishment of the Thirty.[4] In support of this assertion he produces, not the fellow-conspirators of Eratosthenes, but men who had heard him say that he was a member of the committee. He remarks, by way of excuse, that it was impossible to produce original testimony.[5] Doubtless competent witnesses were in court, but, as Lysias suggests, they would not testify by reason of their oath as club members. How far such an oath would be accepted as an excuse we have no means of knowing. It would seem that the law of Demophantus[6] should have released them from the oath.

CHAPTER IV

EXTRAJUDICIAL DEPOSITIONS

Closely connected with hearsay evidence are what may conveniently be called extrajudicial depositions.[7] The evidence of persons who were too ill to attend court, or who were out of the city, could be taken in writing in the presence of a number of persons, who afterward, on the production

[1] D. 41:24.

[2] Isæ. 9:6; on being called in as a witness in another matter, he took the oath of disclaimer, *ibid.*, 18.

[3] D. 34:11, 46. [4] Lys. 12:43 ff. [5] Lys. 12:46. [6] And. 1:98.

[7] "Extrajudicial," because the deposing witness never appeared at any hearing of the case.

of the document in court, by an attesting affidavit identified it as the statement of the original witness. Such testimony then consisted of the extrajudicial deposition and the affidavit of the attesting witness.[1] So far as we know, neither witness was sworn.[2] As the deposition contained the evidence, it was the more important document, and on one occasion at least it is mentioned without any notice of the attesting witness.[3]

Both the deposing and the attesting witnesses were liable to a prosecution for perjury. If the evidence was false, the original witness was liable, unless he could show that he had not made the statement accredited to him. In that case, the attesting witnesses became responsible. In view of possible repudiations by the original witness, it was usual to take his statements in the presence of a large number of reputable persons.[4] In a case in Isæus there is a reference to a repudiation which had evidently been made privately. The matter, however, was not pressed against the attesting witness. The repudiation was merely cited by the speaker in an attempt to throw discredit on the deposition which, contrary to the usual practice, had been taken in presence of only two witnesses.[5]

Platner, relying on the case in Isæus,[6] holds that the statement of the original witness need not be reduced to writing. The language of the lexicographers suggests an oral statement, but is not at all inconsistent with a written statement.[7] The practice of Demosthenes and Æschines,[8] however, was undoubtedly to have the statement reduced to writing. And, indeed, if it were otherwise, it would have been impossible to prosecute the original witness for perjury.

The responsibility of the deposing witness clearly differentiates this class of evidence from hearsay evidence. The person who was the source of the hearsay statement recited in an affidavit was never responsible; the attesting witness alone was held accountable, even when the original witness was still alive.[9] It is true that the lexicographers seem to identify extrajudicial depositions with hearsay, but Demosthenes carefully differ-

[1] Æsch., *De F. L.*, 19; D. 46:7.

[2] Heffter, p. 309.

[3] D. 35:20; cf. Platner, Vol. II, p. 226.

[4] Isæ. 3:20.

[5] Isæ. 3:18.

[6] Isæ. 3:18 ff.

[7] Schol. on Æsch., *De F. L.*, 19; *Lex. Seg.*, Bekker, *Anecdota*, p. 248.

[8] D. 46:7, 8; Æsch., *De F. L.*, p. 19.

[9] Demosthenes does propose to hold Phormio, a party in the suit, responsible for giving evidence in his own behalf, because he was the real source of the evidence of Stephanus, who was being prosecuted for perjury; but he can scarcely be serious in his proposal (D. 46:9 ff.).

entiates them.[1] In one passage, however, ἐκμαρτυρία is loosely used of a kind of evidence which is unquestionably hearsay. It is applied to evidence of the acts of a deceased person whereby he had virtually refused to recognize one who claimed to be his daughter.[2]

This arrangement for securing the evidence of witnesses who could not be present has its counterpart in British and American statute law providing for the appointment of a commission to take the evidence of persons who are out of the jurisdiction of the court or about to leave the jurisdiction or who are sick and unable to attend. The main difference is that in Athens the securing of the depositions was the business of the parties themselves, while with us the court, on the motion of the party interested, authorizes the procuring of the evidence.[3]

CHAPTER V

COMPETENCY OF WITNESSES

In respect of citizens, those only were competent witnesses who were adult males in full possession of their civic rights, and were not parties to the litigation. A free alien could, with one possible exception, be a witness.[4] Thus parties to a suit, women, children, and slaves were excluded. That all of these persons did often come into court in a capacity only technically distinguishable from that of regular witnesses will appear in a more detailed discussion.

These regulations compare favorably with the common-law rules, which excluded the evidence of a party in his own behalf, the evidence of husband and wife in respect of each other, and the evidence of a child if it appeared upon examination by the judge that he did not comprehend the nature and effect of an oath. A party could refuse also to testify for his opponent. In the southern states slaves were not competent witnesses against white men. "Any negro or mulatto, bond or free, shall be a good witness in pleas of the commonwealth for or against negroes or mulattoes,

[1] *Pollux*, VIII, 36; Schol. on Æsch., *De F. L.*, 19; *Lex. Seg.*, Bekker, *Anecdota*, p. 248; D. 46:7; cf. Kennedy, in Smith, *Dictionary of Antiquities*, *s. v.* "ecmartyria," and M. S. L., p. 879.

[2] Isæ. 3:77; cf. Isæ. 8:6, 14 ff., where similar evidence is given. Cf. p. 23.

[3] *U. S. Revised Statutes*, §§ 863 ff.; cf. Greenleaf, Vol. I. §§ 320 ff.

[4] M. S. L., pp. 847, 875; Rentzsch, p. 11; cf. D. 46:9 ff.; 40:58; 59:27, 28; Telfy, art. 684.

bond or free, or in civil pleas where free negroes or mulattoes shall alone be parties, and in no other cases whatsoever."[1] It will be noted that no negro or mulatto, even if free, could appear for or against a white man. Parties are now usually competent, but not compellable, witnesses against themselves in criminal cases, and both competent and compellable in civil cases. In some jurisdictions[2] a person who has been convicted of certain specified crimes is not a competent witness, while in others even a condemned murderer may be called upon to give evidence.

But incompetency may result from special circumstances. An instance occurs in a case before the Areopagus, where all witnesses were required to swear to the truth or falsity of the main charge. The defendant, who was charged with wounding with intent, was unable to prove a fact which went to show that he had become reconciled to the plaintiff, and thus was without malice, because the only witnesses who were aware of it were unable to take the oath required. Thus ignorance of the guilt or innocence of a defendant before the Areopagus disqualified an otherwise competent witness from appearing at all on the case.[3]

INCOMPETENT WITNESSES

1. *Parties interested in the suit.*—"Those are witnesses," says Demosthenes, "who have no interest in the case."[4] Our means for judging of the nature of the interest are limited. Relatives were competent witnesses; and the same person could be both advocate and witness for a friend or a relative.[5] Demosthenes protests against the evidence of a witness on the ground that he is an interested party, but it is impossible to determine from the speech the exact nature of the interest.[6]

In a bottomry case, the defendant, Phormio, had borrowed money from the plaintiff. He alleged that he had intrusted the principal and interest to the captain of a ship at Bosphorus, to be paid to the plaintiff. At first the captain denied receiving the money, and, on the strength of the denial, the plaintiff sued Phormio. When the case came before a private arbitrator, the captain retracted his former statement and admitted the receipt of the money. Now, he certainly had a financial interest in the case, for if Phormio succeeded in resisting the claim of his creditor, the captain would be liable for the amount. Whether he could escape liability by proving that he lost the money in the shipwreck we cannot tell. At any rate, if he received

[1] "Acts of Virginia General Assembly" (*Code*, Vol. I), 1814, ch. 283, 4.

[2] *Revised Statutes of Florida* (1892), Vol. II, § 1096.

[3] Lys. 4:4.

[4] D. 40: 58.

[5] Æsch., *De F. L.*, 170, 184. Isæ. 12:1, 4.

[6] D. 40:58.

the money, he must have been *prima facie* liable to whichever party lost the suit, and yet, so far is the plaintiff from objecting to the evidence of the captain that he actually complains that his affidavit was not submitted to the jury.[1]

In another bottomry case, Protus, a merchant, borrowed money from Demon, an Athenian money-lender, and bought corn in Syracuse. On the arrival of the ship in Athens a third party, Zenothemis, laid claim to the cargo on the ground that it had been mortgaged to him by the captain, who was drowned on the homeward voyage. Demon took possession, and Zenothemis brought suit against him. Demon proposed to call Protus and compel him to give evidence.[2] Now, Protus undoubtedly had an interest in the suit, for if Zenothemis was awarded the cargo, Demon would have had recourse to Protus for the repayment of his loan. Whether he could have succeeded or not is immaterial.

Under these circumstances, it would be unwise to attach much importance to the protest of Demosthenes against a witness on the ground of interest. In practice at least, no one was prevented from appearing as a witness by reason of interest, unless he was actually a party to the suit, and even then he was allowed in inheritance cases to put in an affidavit (διαμαρτυρία) that the estate of the deceased was not subject to litigation on the ground that there was legitimate issue of the deceased alive.[3] The representatives of women or children were allowed to make a διαμαρτυρία under the same circumstances. The affiant in these cases was liable to a δίκη ψευδομαρτυριῶν,[4] and is thus actually a witness in his own behalf.

The failure of a party to appear,[5] or his confession in court or before the Eleven, was sufficient evidence for a verdict.[6] But if the verdict went against a man by default, he could appeal.[7] There is no mention in our authorities of confessions made out of court, which in English practice must be made freely, without any inducement being held out by anyone in authority. The prosecution in the Herodes[8] murder trial produced a letter in which the defendant announced to another that he had accomplished the

[1] D. 34:11, 46. [2] D. 32:30.

[3] D. 44:54, 55; cf. M. S. L., p. 847, n. 227. It is possible that Demosthenes is not stating an actual rule of law, but is merely seeking to discredit the testimony on the ground of interest. Telfy, however (§ 682), treats it as a rule of law, as does Dareste in his translation. Kennedy's rendering preserves the ambiguity of the Greek.

[4] Isæ. 3:3. [5] Lyc. 117; D. 21:81.

[6] Arist., *Const. of Ath.*, 52:1, with Sandys' note, where other passages are cited; cf. Lys. 6:24; 22:7.

[7] M. S. L., pp. 973 ff. [8] Ant. 5:53 ff.

crime. Such a letter, if genuine, would be conclusive proof, but in this case the defendant said it was a forgery. There is also a proposal in the step-mother murder trial to prove, by putting the slaves to torture,[1] that a woman admitted that she had administered poison to her husband. If one who was summarily arrested and taken before the Eleven confessed, he was executed without trial. This is quite contrary to English law, which requires that even a confessed murderer be regularly tried; but one who pleads guilty may be sentenced forthwith.

It was open to any one of several defendants in a criminal case to become an informer and give evidence.[2] Andocides was said to have thus turned informer against his companions in the matter of the mutilation of the Hermæ. Apart from these exceptions to the rule excluding the evidence of parties, a good deal of evidentiary matter is found in the speeches of the litigants. These speeches differ materially from the addresses and arguments of modern lawyers.

As a rule, an Athenian was required to take his own case, though his speech was usually prepared for him by a professional speech-writer who was more or less familiar with the law and the practice. In English courts a man has the privilege of arguing his own case; but it is seldom that he avails himself of it. In Athens the jury looked to the speaker for the facts, and to the witnesses for the corroboration; with us the jury looks to the witnesses for the facts, and to the lawyers for an outline of the case and explanations of the evidence.[3] The reading of the evidence submitted to an Athenian jury would give one but a meager notion of the facts in the case, while a careful reader of the evidence presented to an English jury would be in full possession of all the facts. It is to be expected, however, that a man will sometimes find himself in such a position that he can offer no evidence. And so there occasionally occur cases in which nothing but the bare speech was before the jury.[4] That juries did believe the unsupported statements contained in a speech is clear from a case in Demosthenes.[5] The virtual evidentiary character of addresses in court was thoroughly understood. Speeches are often prefaced by promises to tell the whole truth, or by complaints that the speaker, by reason of his youth or absence from the city at a certain time, is hampered in presenting

[1] Ant. 1:9.

[2] Cf. p. 38.

[3] This was not always the case. As long as the personal knowledge of the jury was recognized as a proper basis for a verdict, we find the allegations of counsel treated as evidence. These conditions continued in England until the beginning of the eighteenth century. Thayer, *Evid.*, pp. 120, 170.

[4] A well-known instance is Isoc. 21.

[5] D. 43:30.

the case by lack of first-hand knowledge of the facts.[1] One of Isocrates' clients, with the purpose of discrediting his opponent's statements, introduced evidence to show that on a previous occasion he had been guilty of perjury.[2] Demosthenes even argues that the law against hearsay evidence ought in justice to be observed by prosecutors in their speeches.[3] The practice of swearing to pleadings was some check on false statements, even though the oaths were formal and did not render one liable to a prosecution of any kind.[4]

An analysis of the speeches of the Orators reveals the fact that certain matters were regularly incorporated in them without corroborative evidence. As a person could not produce the evidence of his own slaves, even if elicited by torture, it was the regular practice to tell the jury what he had learned from them.[5] An excellent example of this occurs in Lysias, where the defendant, on trial for the murder of his wife's paramour, Eratosthenes, tells very dramatically how he questioned a maid-servant and learned the details of his wife's infidelity.[6] Sometimes the recital was accompanied by a challenge to the opponent to torture the slave.[7] If the slave was the property of the other party, a challenge to produce the slave for torture was accompanied by an account of what he was confident the torture would reveal. The plaintiff in the case against his stepmother who was accused of poisoning her husband challenges her to give up her slaves for torture. As the challenge was refused, he goes on to state that the slaves well knew that she had on several occasions been caught in the act of administering poison[8] to her husband. In this way the speaker could practically, though not technically, give evidence of what women or children could prove.[9] Sometimes the excuse of a challenge was lacking.[10] A challenge to give or accept an evidentiary oath also gave an excuse to dispense with corroborative testimony which could not be procured.[11] To give weight to a hearsay statement, Demosthenes on one occasion called down an imprecation on his head, if it were not true.[12] Here properly belongs Demosthenes' offer to testify to the truth of a statement under the same liability as a regular witness.[13] There is no need for supposing[14] that a party had a right under

[1] D. 27:2, 3; 38:6. And. 1:55; Ant. 5:74; 6:14; Lys. 1:5; 31:4.

[2] Isoc. 18:52, 57.

[3] D. 57:4; cf. Lys. 5:4.

[4] Ant. 6:14; D. 33:14; And. 1:55; but cf. Ant. 1:28.

[5] Cf. p. 70.

[6] Lys. 1:18 ff.

[7] D. 29:11 ff.

[8] Ant. 1:9; cf. Lys. 4:10.

[9] D. 55:23, 27.

[10] D. 47:56.

[11] Cf. p. 76.

[12] D. 55:24.

[13] D. *De F. L.*, 176.

[14] M. S. L., p. 877, n. 313.

certain circumstances to testify in his own behalf. This offer is really a challenge. If Æschines had been willing to accept it, Demosthenes might quite properly have given testimony.

As no evidence of what happened subsequently to an arbitration, as a rule, could be produced, such matters were brought before the jury without corroboration. Witnesses in cases before the Areopagus could not testify at all, unless they could swear to the truth or falsity of the indictment. This restriction often deprived a speaker of corroborative evidence of matters which, though not immediately connected with the charge in the indictment, were pertinent to the case.[1]

Another kind of party evidence is sometimes found where the jury's knowledge of the truth of the statement is appealed to as sufficient corroboration. That this practice was often abused by a wily speaker is apparent from Demosthenes' warning to the jurors to be sure that each one of them is in fact aware of the truth of the statement. He says that those who have nothing truthful to say and no witnesses to produce are accustomed to resort to this trick.[2]

An exceptional case is found in Antiphon,[3] where the same person is practically both prosecutor and witness. In his youth he had been the recipient of his father's dying declaration, according to law. On reaching his majority, he prosecuted his stepmother and reported his father's ante-mortem statement.[4]

2. *Women.*—A woman could appear in court neither as a witness nor as a party.[5] If she was a party to any litigation, she was required to appear by her representative (*κύριος*). There was, however, no objection to her being present in court, if she chose.[6] The hardship that would have been caused in many cases by entirely excluding the evidence of women was considerably mitigated by various expedients which were well known to the Orators; so that a litigant always expected to be able to avail himself of the evidence of his female relatives.[7]

In a meeting of relatives to discuss and settle a matter in dispute women were as free to take part as men.[8] In private arbitrations, also, a woman

[1] Lys. 4:4. Cf. *supra*, p. 28.

[2] D. 40:53.

[3] Ant. 1:29 ff.

[4] See p. 21 for a detailed discussion.

[5] M. S. L., p. 876. Isocrates' production of a woman in court to show that she was not dead, as many witnesses had testified, is not an exception to the rule (Isoc. 18:54; cf. p. 81). Plato was in favor of allowing a woman to testify if she were over forty years of age (*Laws*, XI, 937, A).

[6] D. 59:14. Hyperides (*Frag.* 60) went so far on one occasion, it is said, as to display to the jurors the charms of his client Phryne in order to win their compassion.

[7] D. 38:6; 36:14.

[8] Lys. 32:12 ff.

was permitted to appear and tell what she knew.[1] In inheritance cases her representative could take an affidavit (διαμαρτυρία) that the action was not maintainable,[2] and the woman herself might in any kind of suit take an evidentiary oath, if the other party agreed.[3] The result was acccpted as final.

Another common means of getting a woman's statements before the jury was to incorporate them in the speech.[4] As pains were always taken to mention that the woman was in a position to know the facts, the plan was, on the whole, fairly effective in impressing the jury. Demosthenes, in his suit against Aphobus, quotes his mother as his authority for the contents of his father's will.[5] He makes no offer of her evidentiary oath, but in a later speech against Aphobus he brought evidence to show that she was willing to swear on the heads of her children that her husband had on his death-bed manumitted a certain Milyas.[6] The speaker might emphasize his recital of what he had learned from a woman by an imprecation on his own head, if he were not telling the truth.[7]

In matters of pedigree and family history secondary evidence of the declarations of a deceased female relative was admissible.[8] The account-books and other business papers of a deceased female, or even a paper prepared especially in presence of witnesses for the purpose of charging a certain person with a debt, could be submitted to the jury.[9] It was the regular practice to admit, by way of hearsay evidence, the admissions of a party to a suit.[10] There is an instance of the extension of this rule so as to include the admissions of the wife of a party.[11]

Occasionally men were called upon to give evidence which, in part at least, was virtually hearsay from their wives. A certain Euphiletus had appealed against the decision of his deme, which had deprived him of his citizenship. Among others, his brothers-in-law had testified regarding his paternity. His half-brother, who was his representative, in seeking to show the reliability of this evidence, recalls the natural prejudice that exists between stepmothers and stepdaughters, and then adds: "If anyone else than our father had been the father of the plaintiff, our stepmother's son, my sisters would not have permitted their husbands to give this testimony."[12]

1 D. 59:46. 2 Isæ. 3:3. 3 D. 39:3, 18; 40:41; cf. p. 75.

4 D. 47:56 ff. A later passage in this speech (68 ff.) affords rather plausible grounds for supposing that in murder trials women were permitted to be witnesses. I hope to publish, in a separate article, the arguments that seem to support this view.

5 D. 27:40.

6 D. 29:26.

7 D. 55:24.

8 D. 43:37, 46.

9 D. 41:9.

10 See p. 24.

11 D. 41:24.

12 Isæ. 12:5.

As an informer, a woman had exactly the same status before the courts as a man.[1] A woman was allowed to appear in court to arouse the sympathy of the jurors in behalf of her relatives.[2]

3. *Children.*—The exclusion of the evidence of children[3] was not as inconvenient as in the case of women. Hence we hear of fewer expedients for escaping the provisions of the law. Recourse could be had to a challenge, just as in the case of women. The defendant who was charged with the murder of the chorus boy had previously to the regular accusation been informally charged with the murder in a court where he was a prosecutor. On two successive days, in presence of the jurors and spectators, he challenged the accusers to take witnesses and go to those who were present when the poisoned drink was administered. He said that more than fifty men and boys were present, and he offered to give a list of them.[4]

4. *Slaves.*—The evidence of slaves was admissible only when elicited by torture. A seeming exception occurs when a slave turns informer.[5] An unscrupulous person might possibly pretend that a slave was a freeman and produce him as a witness. At least we hear of one case where it was claimed that slaves were successfully foisted upon the court as freemen.[6] The plea that a slave who was demanded for torture had been set free was of common occurrence. On being set free, a slave was no longer under any disability, as we see in Apollodorus v. Timotheus, where the plaintiff challenges his opponent to give up a certain Æschrion for torture or produce him as a witness.[7]

Those who hold that slaves could give evidence in murder trials rely upon a single passage in Antiphon.[8] But an examination of Antiphon's ordinary use of technical legal terms shows considerable looseness and lack of precision, and suggests caution in recognizing an exception so opposed to Athenian prejudices on the subject of slaves. Legal procedure in general was not so fixed in Antiphon's time as it was in the time of Demosthenes, nor was the terminology so exact. In the same speech Antiphon used ἀπαγωγή loosely of the violent proceedings of the prosecutors in hurrying the defendant to prison without allowing him to give bail, rather

[1] And., *De Myst.*, 16; see p. 39.

[2] D. 48:57.

[3] Telfy, § 684.

[4] Ant. 6:19, 22 ff.

[5] Lys. 5:3 ff.; 7:16; cf. p. 39.

[6] D. 59:9; cf. Lys. 4:14; Isoc. 17:14.

[7] D. 49:55, 56. Platner (Vol. II, p. 216) makes it clear that, if Æschrion was not a slave, he must have been a freedman. His hesitancy to base any conclusion on the passage because the incident occurred before an arbitrator is not justified by the facts; for the plaintiff distinctly contemplates the possibility of having the man's testimony filed.

[8] Ant. 5:48: εἴπερ γὰρ καὶ μαρτυρεῖν ἔξεστι δούλῳ κατὰ τοῦ ἐλευθέρου τὸν φόνον.

than in its strictly technical sense, which would be incompatible with ἔνδειξις.[1] It was inevitable that the technical and the literary signification of words should occasionally be confused. This was particularly true of *μάρτυς* and *μαρτυρεῖν*. By insisting upon the technical meaning of these words in every instance in which they occur, a plausible case for regarding a party to a suit as a witness for his opponent could easily be made out.[2] And Antiphon uses *μαρτυρεῖν* of a man who on his death-bed makes a statement regarding the cause of his death.[3] We are then not surprised to find, as Guggenheim has shown, that he regularly uses the words *μαρτυρία* and *μαρτυρεῖν* of informers.[4]

There are several other considerations that must not be lost sight of in this discussion. Antiphon's statement that a slave could give evidence in a murder trial is, as the lawyers say, a mere dictum, entirely disconnected with any issue in the case. A slave who had sailed with the defendant and Herodes had been tortured into a confession charging the defendant with the murder of Herodes, and was afterward put to death. Antiphon sharply criticises the conduct of the prosecution in putting the slave to death without due process of law. He sums up the rights which a slave in his relations to freemen enjoyed under the law. The slave was protected against assaults of any kind. If they fall short of inflicting mortal injury, his master has a right of action against the assailant. In case the injuries prove fatal, it is murder no less than if he had been a freeman. Besides this protection, the slave enjoyed the privilege of charging a freeman with murder. His conclusion is that, if a slave can charge a freeman with murder, and if a freeman must stand his trial for the murder of a slave, surely it is impossible that a slave can be put to death without trial. Now, this argument is in no wise weakened by limiting *μαρτυρῶ* to mean *μηνύω*. He means simply that a slave can give evidence in the only way in which

[1] Ant. 5:9: *πρῶτον μὲν γὰρ κακοῦργος ἐνδεδειγμένος φόνου δίκην φεύγω.* —— *εἰς ταύτην τὴν ἀπαγωγὴν νομιμωτάτην καὶ δικαιοτάτην πεποιήκασιν ὑμῖν τὴν ἀποψήφισίν μου.* Of Blass, *Attische Beredsamkeit*, Vol. I, p. 176; Jebb, *Attic Orators*, Vol. I, p. 56, note; M. S. L., pp. 277 ff. Those who, like Blass and Lipsius, attempt to explain the passage on the assumption that ἀπαγωγή is used in its technical sense are involved in considerable difficulty. If we regard ἔνδειξις as the information, and ἀπαγωγή as referring simply to the arrest with its aggravating circumstances, we are freed from the necessity of treating this as an exception to the rule that in cases of ἀπαγωγή the penalty was not assessed by the jury (M. S. L., p. 238). A similar confusion between a slave informer and a slave witness prevails throughout the same speech (cf. p. 71). Cf. Sorof, *Neues Jahrbuch für Philologie*, Vol. CXXVII, p. 105; Meuss, *De ἀπαγωγῆς actione apud Athenienses.*

[2] Isæ. 6:12; D. 28:9; Ant. 6:32.

[3] Ant. 1:29.

[4] Guggenheim, pp. 7 ff., has pointed out that the slaves who in Ant. 1:30 are summoned to hear their master's dying declaration are not witnesses, but informers.

the law would accept his voluntary evidence; for an informer is, after all, a witness in a certain sense. Antiphon's reason for selecting murder as the subject in respect to which a slave could lay an information is not because a slave could not be an informer in other matters as well,[1] but because it enabled him to put his objection to the murder of the slave with more telling effect.[2]

Another point to be borne in mind is that the exception applies only in case the evidence of the slave is against a supposed murderer. This is suspiciously like an information which of necessity could never be in favor of a man except indirectly. It would seem to us to be quite as important, if a slave was to be a witness at all, to have him give evidence in behalf of a man charged with murder as well as against him. What a valuable witness the slave girl would have been in behalf of her master charged with the murder of Eratosthenes.[3]

It is pertinent to this discussion to inquire how the testimony (μαρτυρία) of a regular witness is to be distinguished from an information (μήνυσις), on the one hand, and from statements elicited by torture (βάσανοι), on the other. A regular witness was obliged to attend in court when summoned, and to take an oath, always in murder cases, and in other cases probably at the option of the other side. In case of refusal to appear and testify, the witness might render himself liable to a suit for failure to give evidence, or to a suit for damages, or even to a fine.[4] Neither oaths nor any of these suits are ever mentioned in connection with an informer or a slave handed over to torture.[5] The informer appeared willingly in the first instance, and was exempted from all legal liability in connection with his information,[6] while a slave was always under constraint, and obliged to appear when required. Thus regular testimony is distinguished from information and slave testimony chiefly by reason of the liability to these several actions and the obligation to take a solemn oath.

The Athenian law made a master responsible for the actions of his slaves to the extent of paying fines and debts incurred by them.[7] Thus the machinery of law provided a means for obtaining from a master redress if a slave, being required to appear as a witness, failed to testify. But there are several considerations which make it extremely improbable that a slave could be required to appear as a witness in a murder trial. As a rule, a master was not obliged to give up his slave for examination, however important his evidence might be, to his opponent in a suit, or even to a

[1] Lys. 5:5; 7:17; Ant. 1:11.

[2] Ant. 5:48.

[3] Lys. 1:18.

[4] Cf. p. 41.

[5] Cf. pp. 38, 69.

[6] Cf. p. 41.

[7] Hyper. 5:22; cf. Beauchet, Vol. II, pp. 425 ff.

third party, in circumstances under which the master could be subjected to no possible loss; for the loss of the slave's service was borne by the party who examined him.[1] If, then, a master could not be forced to give up his slave to be questioned in cases where his interests could in no way be prejudiced either by the injuries suffered by the slave or by the disclosures he might make, it is difficult to understand how any citizen could compel the attendance of any and every slave he might require in prosecuting one accused of murder. And the hardship would have been increased if the person thus requiring the slave could hold the master liable for any default of the slave. The conclusion that there were no means of compelling the attendance of a slave under these circumstances seems unavoidable. Thus one of the chief characteristics of a witness disappears, and the slave is in this respect in no wise distinguishable from an informer.

Moreover, a passage in Antiphon[2] strongly suggests that a slave could not be a witness. The defendant, who was charged with the murder of a chorus boy, challenged the prosecution to leave the question to the evidence of those who were present, and offered to try to induce their masters to allow the slaves to be tortured, in case it seemed desirable. If the slaves could be witnesses subject to summons, what need to persuade their owners to allow them to be tortured, or why should they be tortured at all rather than be put on their oath?

The same difficulties present themselves in connection with perjury, as Rentzsch admits.[3] The assumption that the same procedure was followed as Plato recommends[4] is not satisfactory; for it again puts the slave on a different footing from that of a freeman by requiring a surety for his appearance in court in case of his being accused of perjury. It is hardly necessary, however, to remark that Plato's regulations permitting a slave to testify afford no presumption in favor of a similar rule in Athenian law.

In regard to the administering of an oath to a slave, Antiphon himself seems to deny the possibility of such a proceeding. In a statement of the means available for guaranteeing the truth of evidence, he puts in distinct contrast oaths and pledges for freemen, and other means of compulsion for slaves,[5] and that, too, in a murder trial. When we recollect that he

[1] And. 1:22, 64; cf. Mahaffy, *Social Life in Greece*, p. 241.

[2] Ant. 6:22 ff.

[3] Rentzsch, p. 16, n. 20.

[4] Plato, *Laws*, 937 A.

[5] Ant. 6:25. Rentzsch (p. 16), without apparent warrant, concludes that slaves could give evidence without being sworn, if a surety was produced; cf. Plato, *Laws*, XI, 937, B.

is delivering a speech in defense of a suspected murderer, against whom these slaves might have been used as witnesses, if the usual interpretation of *μαρτυρῶ* is correct, the passage is significant. And in this respect also the slave resembles an informer, who was not put on oath, rather than a witness, who was always sworn in murder trials.

Furthermore, it is remarkable that there is no reference to slaves as actual witnesses in connection with the half-dozen murders that are mentioned in the Orators.[1] This can scarcely have been the result of chance, as in at least three of these cases slaves were in possession of information that would have been valuable to the prosecution.[2] The slave who was brought before the jury in Nicobulus v. Pantænetus[3] to show that he was incapable by reason of weakness of committing the assault charged, had a certain evidentiary value as real evidence;[4] but this does not constitute an exception to the rule that a slave could not be a witness.

If, then, a slave could not be compelled to appear in court, or be proceeded against in the ordinary way in case of perjury, to say nothing of the apparent impossibility of administering a solemn oath to him, he cannot properly be called a witness; and only confusion can result from calling him a witness, when the chief essentials of regular testimony are lacking, and all the essentials of an information are present.

CHAPTER VI

INFORMERS

The informer (*μηνυτής*) included both the Roman "delator" and the accomplice who in English practice is said to turn king's, queen's, or state's evidence; but the term is most widely used of a slave who, having become aware of a crime committed by his master, informs upon him.[5] Batrachus and Æschylides were typical delators under the Thirty.[6] Informers were protected against any prosecution to which they might have rendered themselves liable by a grant of immunity.[7] Only the senate or the assembly could grant such immunity. The case of the committee of senators which promised immunity to Agoratus[8] is quite exceptional.

The practice was simple. The informer appeared before the senate or the assembly and gave in a list of names (*ἀπογραφή*).[9] The accused might

[1] Ant. 1:9; 5:29, 49; 6:22; Lys. 12; 13; D. 47:68 ff.

[2] Ant. 1; 5; 6.

[3] D. 37:44.

[4] Cf. p. 81.

[5] Lys. 7:16.

[6] Lys. 12:48; cf. And. 1:42.

[7] And. 1:15, 20.

[8] Lys. 13:26.

[9] And. 1:13; Lys. 13:30.

be tried forthwith[1] or handed over to a regular court.[2] It is not certain whether the informer appeared before the court or not.[3]

Any person was competent to become an informer. Among those mentioned by Andocides in connection with the profanation of the Mysteries are a woman,[4] a metic,[5] and a slave.[6] The information of a slave was accepted without torture; but the rack was often used to extort a confession from a suspected criminal slave, and such confessions often implicated others.[7] If the information, however, was given freely, the slave was not tortured, but rather rewarded with freedom. The reward of the freeman was usually in the shape of money.[8]

Andocides cites a law according to which the punishment for false information was death. This has been regarded as a special enactment, applying only to the inquiry regarding the Mysteries and the Hermæ.[9] If it was a general law, a subtle pleader like Antiphon would scarcely have failed to draw the conclusion that the friends of Herodes, in putting the slave to death, practically admitted the falsity of his evidence.[10] Nor would Lysias, in speaking of those who informed against Callias, have said that they had nothing to lose if they failed, and everything to gain if they succeeded.[11]

CHAPTER VII

PROCURING EVIDENCE OF TRANSACTIONS

It was characteristic of the Athenians to rely on witnesses rather than on documents. This often made it difficult to establish a claim when, owing to the lapse of years, the witnesses were dead.[12] It was customary to have witnesses present at almost every kind of transaction, in order that they might be available in the case of subsequent litigation;[13] though frequently, as in the case of challenges, a man would rely on finding wit-

[1] Lys. 13:36, 37.

[2] And. 1:17.

[3] M. S. L., pp. 330–32. The language used of the informer in the Herodes murder trial seems to indicate that if he had not been put to death he would have appeared before the court (Ant. 5:46; cf. p. 71).

[4] And. 1:16.

[5] And. 1:15.

[6] And. 1:11, 27.

[7] Ant. 1:20; cf. *Tetral.*, A, γ, 4.

[8] Ant. 5:34; cf. Plato, *Laws*, XI, 932, D.

[9] M. S. L., pp. 955, n. 544; Grote, *History of Greece*, Vol. VII, p. 174.

[10] Ant. 5:34.

[11] Lys. 5:34.

[12] D. 38:6; cf. 36:17, 27.

[13] Isæ. 3:19.

nesses ready to hand.[1] If he neglected to provide himself with witnesses, he was sometimes obliged to have recourse to men who might prove adverse;[2] while, if no witnesses at all were present at a transaction, it was a matter of suspicion,[3] except in certain well-recognized cases. The most common exceptions are bankers' contracts.[4] The care with which bankers' accounts were kept,[5] and the good repute in which they were generally held, may account for the custom.[6] Wills were almost always reduced to writing.[7] Witnessess were summoned simply to have evidence that the testator had in fact made a will. Of its contents they knew nothing. Indeed, they might find it impossible even to identify the will.[8] Dying declarations in cases of murder were permitted to be oral, if made before friends and relatives; but if made before slaves, they were regularly reduced to writing.[9] Contracts were not required to be written;[10] but suits arising out of maritime contracts could not be brought to the speedy trial especially provided for certain classes of urgent cases, unless the terms of the agreement were reduced to writing.[11]

A multiplicity of witnesses was desirable; but there is no trace of any legal requirement for more than one witness in any particular class of cases, as in English law, except that, as a rule, there were at least two witnesses to a writ of summons.[12] The absence of these requirements is all the more remarkable in comparison with the practice in other states. The law of Gortyn enumerates several cases in which a specified number of witnesses was required.[13] A common modern example is the rule which requires more than one witness to a will, although only one need be called to prove the will. So in the case of treason two witnesses are required.

1 D. 47:12; cf. 47:36.

2 D. 57:14.

3 D. 30:20, 38.

4 Isoc. 17:2.

5 D. 49:5 ff.; 52:6.

6 Isoc. 17:2, 18.

7 A nuncupative or oral will is allowed in English law in certain cases; but it must be reduced to writing within a limited time after the death of the testator; cf. M. S. L., p. 595.

8 Isæ. 4:13, 14.

9 Ant. 1:29, 30.

10 Hyper. 5:13; cf. Beauchet, Vol. IV, p. 46.

11 D. 32:1; but cf. Beauchet, Vol. IV, pp. 93, 319, 323.

12 D. 34:28; 47:44; 48:47; 50:29; Isæ. 3:23, 24; Lys. 12:61; D. 47:12. An inscription found in Decelea some years ago shows that at the introduction of a new member into the phratry three witnesses were required. Simon, *Wiener Studien*, Vol. XII (1890), p. 70.

13 Gilbert, p. 469.

A COMPULSORY PROCESS FOR WITNESSES

The usual difficulties encountered in procuring the attendance of witnesses at the various hearings of a case were often increased by the opposite party, who might employ fear, persuasion, or bribery to induce a witness to absent himself.[1] But the Athenian law provided a varicty of means for obliging a witness to attend. It was always incumbent on a litigant to notify his witnesses to be present at the arbitration or the trial. Witness fees, however, either in the way of remuneration for the time spent in court or for traveling expenses, are quite unknown in Athenian practice. Owing to the meagerness of our authorities, we are often without definite knowledge in respect of many details; and not a few conclusions that have been reached depend very largely upon conjecture.

The leading case is Apollodorus v. Timotheus.[2] Antiphanes, one of the plaintiff's witnesses, had failed to appear and give evidence before the arbitrator, as he had repeatedly promised to do. After vainly summoning the witness from his house, Apollorodus instituted before the arbitrator an action against him for default (δίκη λιπομαρτυρίου), depositing a drachma to be forfeited in case of failure in the suit. The result was that both suits went against Apollodorus. Taking this case along with the notices of the lexicographers,[3] we obtain some definite information as to the nature of the suit.

It could be instituted only in case a witness had pledged himself to be present. A deposit of a drachma was required, and the defaulting witness was liable to a fine, the amount of which was determined by the jury. For anything beyond these facts we have no certain data; but Lipsius very plausibly conjectures that the main suit was delayed until the case against the witness was settled.[4] In the case under discussion, a second suit was brought against the witness to recover damages; but we cannot be certain that such a suit could have been brought, had the action for default been carried to a successful conclusion.

But is it not possible that the δίκη λιπομαρτυρίου was a public suit, in which the fine went to the public treasury? Apollodorus, speaking of the two suits against Antiphanes, especially emphasizes the fact that the action for damages was a private suit,[5] as if in contrast with a public suit (δίκη δημοσία); and the error of Photius in speaking of it as an ἀδίκημα which rendered the offender liable to a public prosecution (ἐφ' ᾧ γραφὴ ἦν),

[1] D. 21:137; 32:29; 44:3; 58:7; Lys. 20:18.

[2] D. 49:19.

[3] Photius, *s. v.* λειπομαρτύριον and λειπομαρτυρίου δίκη; cf. Suidas, *s. v.*

[4] M. S. L., p. 499.

[5] D. 49:20.

may be the result of a confusion between γραφή and δίκη δημοσία. This explanation has the advantage of preserving an analogy between δίκη λιπομαρτυρίου and κλήτευσις, where the fine went to the public treasury. If this view is correct, a damage suit would not be excluded by a successful action for default, from which the litigant could in no event obtain full satisfaction for his loss.

Several other questions which can be answered only by conjecture have been mooted. For example, it is idle to ask whether an action for damages would lie in cases where the party whose witness had failed him was successful in the original suit; for there are many conceivable ways in which loss might have been suffered even where the judgment of the court was favorable. Rentzsch is of the opinion that an action against a witness might secure a new trial of the original suit. He relies solely on the reasonableness of such a provision, and on the analogy with a suit for perjury.[1]

In case a witness who had not promised to give evidence was present in court, the speaker might request the jury to bid him testify[2] or to make some attempt in an entirely informal manner to persuade him to do his duty.[3] If the speaker did not choose to adopt this procedure, which was possible only when the witness was present, he could have him summoned in a formal manner (κλήτευσις).[4] An inquiry was thereupon instituted by the court, with the object of forcing the witness either to give evidence or to take the oath of disclaimer. If he refused to do either, the court might impose a fine of one thousand drachmas, which went to the public treasury.[5]

This practice is analogous to proceedings in contempt of court in English law, where the offender is summarily fined or imprisoned by the court before which the offense is committed. Thus, if a witness who has been regularly subpœnaed refuses to answer proper questions, he can be forthwith imprisoned for contempt of court; and, in the same way, if the witness refuses to appear, the court may issue a bench warrant for his arrest, and proceed to exact the penalties for failure to comply with the command of the court. In English practice the court takes the initiative in securing the attendance and answers of witnesses, while in Athenian courts the party himself had to move in the matter.[6]

It remains to consider whether a suit for damages would lie in cases where the witness had already been subjected to a fine of one thousand

[1] Rentzsch, p. 22. [2] D. 58:7, 26.

[3] Lyc., *Leoc.*, 20. [4] Pollux 8:36–37. [5] Æsch. *Tim.*, 46.

[6] An English litigant may institute a civil suit for damages if he has suffered by the default of a witness (Masterman v. Judson, 4 Bingham 224).

drachmas. There is no evidence of such a possibility. But if, as has been suggested,[1] a damage suit could be resorted to against an unpledged witness instead of κλήτευσις, it would be reasonable to suppose that the fine would not in any way interfere with the right to bring action for the damage suffered. Naturally κλήτευσις was available also in cases where the witness had pledged himself to appear,[2] and would be an alternative to an action for default, with the distinction that κλήτευσις could not be used against a witness who failed to appear before an arbitrator.

Witnesses who were compelled to go on the stand could still escape giving testimony by swearing that they knew nothing about the matter before the court, if they had the hardihood to take the solemn oath required in such cases.[3] No liability was attached to a false oath of disclaimer. As no evidence had been given by the witness, he could not be proceeded against for perjury. Nor was he liable to an action for damages, even if it could be proved that he did in fact have information on the subject-matter of the suit. Apollodorus, in his suit against Timotheus,[4] says that, as the witness Antiphanes had neither given evidence nor taken the oath of disclaimer, he had instituted a suit for damages against him. It is implied that, had he taken the oath of disclaimer, he would have been free from all liability. This conclusion is further strengthened by the language of Pollux, who says that a witness who refused to give testimony, or to take the oath of disclaimer, was liable to a fine.[5]

Our means for judging of the effectiveness of this machinery are rather meager. On several occasions in the Orators, witnesses are mentioned who were likely to prove refractory, but finally yielded to a threat.[6] Demosthenes, having brought an action for damages against a witness who had failed him at an arbitration, calls him later, when the same matter was before a regular court. It is not distinctly stated that the witness profited by his former experience and gave his testimony.[7] The tone of Demosthenes in one passage does not show entire confidence in the willingness of the court to aid him in compelling the attendance of the witnesses.[8]

WITNESSES COMPETENT, BUT NOT COMPELLABLE

English courts do not require a witness to give evidence that will incriminate himself, or, in some jurisdictions, tend to disgrace him.[9] Apparently a similar rule was observed at Athens. Æschines on one occasion, in an

[1] Rentzsch, p. 23.
[2] D. 32:29, 30.
[3] D. 45:60 ff.; Lyc. 1:20.
[4] D. 49:20.
[5] Pollux 8:37.
[6] D. 58:42 ff.; 59:84; Lyc. I:20.
[7] D. 49:20. Rentzsch, p. 24, believes that the witness did testify. Cf. p. 78.
[8] D. 58:7.
[9] Southard v. Rexford, 6 Cowen 254. Greenleaf, I, § 469 d.

attempt to induce a witness to testify to certain immoral relations that had existed between himself and the defendant Timarchus in his boyhood, says: "What I have written down for you is the truth, but it is carefully composed. I have not given a name to your relationship with the defendant, nor have I put down anything that would expose a truthful witness to any legal liability. . . . . The evidence is neither dangerous nor disgraceful to the witness."[1]

The Athenian law of slander recognized no exception in the case of statements made by anyone in the course of legal proceedings. Such statements, according to English law, are privileged, if relevant.[2] There is an Athenian case in which a witness in a suit afterward sued the prosecutor, who had in court charged him with the murder of his own father. To say that one was a murderer, or that he had thrown away his shield, or to speak ill of the dead,[3] was actionable (ἀπόρρητα). Naturally a witness would be equally liable, and might properly refuse to give evidence that would expose himself to an action for slander.[4]

It would seem, too, that a witness was not required to give evidence that would necessitate the breaking of an oath. Lysias admits the impossibility of forcing members of the political clubs (ἑταιρεῖαι) to give evidence in contravention of their oath as club members.[5]

An exception was allowed, too, in the case of a witness who had been twice convicted of giving false testimony; he could refuse to appear as a witness in any subsequent proceedings. The reason, according to Hyperides, was the reluctance of the state to expose a man to the possible loss of civic rights,[6] which followed a third conviction for perjury.

Still another exemption from the duty of giving evidence was perhaps granted to young men who had just been enrolled as citizens. These young men, during their two years of probation, did not appear in the courts either as defendants or as plaintiffs, except in lawsuits connected with the estates to which they had some claim. It follows from this that they probably would not ordinarily be required to appear in court as witnesses.[7]

[1] Æsch. 1:45.

[2] Pollock, *Torts*, p. 330.

[3] Lys. 10:1 ff., 9; cf. D. 20:104; Plutarch, *Solon*, 21; Isoc. 20:3.

[4] The truth of the statement was a good defense in an action for slander. Athenian law knows nothing of the English rule, "The greater the truth, the greater the libel," which prevails if the aggrieved party seeks redress by means of a criminal prosecution.

[5] Lys. 12:43, 47; cf. Frohberger's note, and cf. Lys. 13:21, 22. Cf. *supra*, p. 25.

[6] Hyper., 4:12; cf. Plato, *Laws*, 937 B.

[7] Arist., *Const. of Athens*, 42:5.

Some doubt exists as to the possibility of compelling relatives of either of the parties to testify. They were, of course, competent witnesses. Two cases can be cited to uphold the view that they were not compellable witnesses. The relatives of Timotheus successfully refused, on the ground of relationship, to testify against him;[1] and in one of Isæus' cases the speaker promised to produce the arbitrators themselves to prove their own award, if they were willing to give evidence. The proviso was added because they were related to the defendants.[2] In support of these cases we may point to the strong feeling on the part of the Greeks on the subject of testifying against one's own relations. To this feeling Apollodorus appeals in his case against Stephanus, where Deinias, a witness, is commended for refusing to give evidence that would be detrimental to his kinsman, the defendant. As the witness apparently took the oath of disclaimer, we may fairly conclude that he knew nothing about the case. But Apollodorus, for his own purposes, assumes that he refused to give evidence that would be detrimental to his relative, and pretends to respect his position. According to the view of Apollodorus, he must have taken a false oath of disclaimer to avoid appearing as a witness. The noteworthy point about the incident is that he trusted that the jury would approve of the course of Deinias.[3] In the same strain is a previous statement that, while perjury is deserving of severe condemnation in any case, it is all the more reprehensible when it is against a relative.[4] These cases would be conclusive, were it not for an incident in Aphobus v. Phanus.[5] Aphobus, it is alleged by the speaker, had been forced in a previous case to give evidence against a relative. But this is an *ex parte* statement, and, in the absence of an explanation of the circumstances from the standpoint of Aphobus, it is not wise to base any conclusion on this case,[6] particularly when there are several instances in which a litigant claimed that he could not secure the testimony of certain witnesses because of their relationship to his opponent. And, furthermore, the Greek feeling on the question of relationship, so well illustrated by the remarks of Apollodorus already cited, would scarcely tolerate the use of compulsion.

1 D. 49:38. Relatives include those related by marriage (D. 45:53 ff.).

2 Isæ. 2:33.

3 D. 45:56, with Sandys' note.

4 D. 45:53.

5 D. 29:19 ff.

6 Cf. Platner, Vol. II, p. 218.

CHAPTER VIII

WRITTEN AND ORAL EVIDENCE

Demosthenes states very explicitly that all evidence had to be reduced to writing and presented to the courts in the form of affidavits.[1] His language affords no clue as to the date of the law. It is plain, however, from the speeches of the later Orators that it was in force at least from the time of Isæus. For the earlier period there is nothing in the speeches themselves that would suggest written evidence, even to the most attentive reader who has no preconceived notions on the subject.[2] But, curiously enough, it has generally been assumed that the evidence was regularly reduced to writing throughout the entire period covered by the extant speeches.

On introducing the evidence of witnesses, the predecessors of Isæus invariably summoned the witness to come forward.[3] As the clerk of the court was accustomed to read to the jury written evidentiary matter, such as laws and decrees, it is remarkable that the speakers never by any chance called for the reading of the depositions, as they commonly did in the later period, particularly when the two classes of evidence are produced at the same time.[4] It is true that, as the presence of witnesses was required in court except in certain specified cases, a request to summon a witness is not out of place even when his evidence was in writing; but it is remarkable that the expression was not occasionally varied so as to apply both to the summoning of a witness and to the reading of his evidence, as was the case later.[5] Nor is there a single instance where the language is inconsistent with oral evidence.[6]

But, apart from this negative proof, drawn from the language of the speakers, there are undoubted instances of the introduction of oral evidence. Andocides actually questions a witness in the presence of the jury;[7] and

[1] D. 45:44; 47:48; M. S. L., p. 884.

[2] M. S. L., p. 495, n. 55.

[3] E. g., *κάλει μοι τοὺς μάρτυρας. τοὺς μάρτυρας παρέξομαι.* Cf. *τῶν μαρτύρων ἀκηκόατε.*

[4] Cf. Lys. 17:8, where the calling of witnesses and the reading of a document are clearly differentiated by the language used: *μάρτυρας ὑμῖν παρέξομαι, ἀναγνωσθήσονται δὲ ὑμῖν καὶ αὗται αἱ ἀπογραφαί.*

[5] E. g., *καί μοι τούτους κάλει καὶ τὰς μαρτυρίας ἀνάγνωθι.*

[6] **Μαρτυρία** is used by Lysias only twice, by Isocrates once, and in neither case does it necessarily mean a written deposition: Lys. 4:12; 20:18; Isoc. 18:56.

[7] And. 1:14.

throughout the speech on the Mysteries his language in bringing forward witnesses seems quite incompatible with written depositions.[1] So Lysias also used language, on some occasions, that seems to exclude the possibility of written evidence.[2]

It may be noted here that the practice of reducing other matters to writing was not so prevalent in the earlier period; laws were often incorporated in the speech, or briefly summarized, and challenges were never written.[3]

When, however, we reach the speeches of Isæus and Demosthenes, the formulas for introducing evidence suddenly change, and the reference to written evidence is beyond question. The earlier expressions are still used; occasionally there is mention both of the summoning of the witness and of the reading of the affidavit.[4] This mixing of expressions is due to the fact that, as the witness was always present in court, it is proper to speak of summoning him. The most natural way of accounting for this state of affairs is to assume that the law requiring evidence to be reduced to writing was not in force during the entire period embraced by the extant orations. It was later than 380 B. C., when the public career of Lysias was ended, and earlier than the bulk of the speeches of Isæus.[5]

Written evidence is an unusual form in which to lay testimony before a jury, and certainly the practice was not introduced without some special object in view. It is perhaps significant that Demosthenes speaks of written evidence in connection with a perjury case. Evidence was written, he said, to prevent any change being made. Possibly the practice in connection with arbitration may have suggested the easiest means of holding the witness responsible for what he actually said. It is not necessary to suppose that it was part of the law providing for the institution of proceedings

1 And. 1:18: *βλέπετε εἰς τούτους, καὶ μαρτυρεῖτε εἰ ἀληθῆ λέγω.* 69, *αὐτοὺς κάλει . . . μέχρι τούτου ἀναβήσονται καὶ λέξουσιν ὑμῖν, ἕως ἂν ἀκροᾶσθαι βούλησθε.* 112, *καί μοι κάλει αὐτόν. πρῶτα μὲν οὖν ταῦτα εἰ ἀληθῆ λέγω μαρτύρησον.*

2 *Οἱ μᾶλλόν τε ἐμοῦ εἰδότες καὶ παραγεγενημένοι οἷς ἐκεῖνος ἔπραττε διηγήσονται καὶ μαρτυρήσονται.*—Lysias 17:2.

3 Ant. 5:9, 12; And. 1:95; Lys. 4:15; 7:34; cf. Isoc. 17:53 ff., where an important challenge is discussed; Ant. 1:6 ff.; 6:24.

4 Isæ. 6:11.

5 There is no reference to written evidence in the first speech of Isæus, nor in the tenth, and there is no reason why these may not have been the earliest of his speeches. The fifth is usually regarded as the earliest speech, but it may be as late as 372 (Jebb, Vol. II, p. 351). Blass (Vol. II, p. 531) puts the first speech among the later solely on the ground of the avoidance of hiatus; but, as Jebb (Vol. II, pp. 320, 328) points out, this method of dating a speech is not entirely reliable.

against false witnesses.[1] It is impossible to fix, even approximately, the date of such an innovation; but it was probably later than the institution of compulsory arbitration, which, in any event, was earlier than the public career of Isæus.[2] When the decision of an arbitrator was made subject to review by the higher court, written evidence was naturally required. The advantages of this system in facilitating proceedings for perjury would easily account for its extension so as to include cases sent directly to trial by the magistrate.

The point at which the evidence was reduced to writing, according to the generally accepted view, was at the preliminary investigation, in cases where arbitration was not compulsory; otherwise the affidavits were filed with the arbitrator.[3] "Die kunstlosen Beweise aber," says Lipsius, "mussten in der Regel alle schriftlich zu den Acten gelegt werden und deshalb nothwendig schon bei der Anakrisis vorkommen."[4] And in a later chapter he remarks: "Der Ausdruck 'eine Schrift in den Echinos legen' so viel bedeutet als 'sie in der Anakrisis zu den Acten bringen.'"[5] Dr. Sandys has challenged this view, on the ground that ἐχῖνος, the official evidence box, is never associated with the ἀνάκρισις by Aristotle, or by any one of the lexicographers or scholiasts. Nor is there in the Orators a single indubitable example of ἐχῖνος, except in connection with arbitration.[6] A careful examination of all the passages in which the technical words used in connection with the filing of documents with an arbitrator occur, fails to disclose a single instance in which these words are connected with the ἀνάκρισις. In several cases they are distinctly connected with an arbitration.[7] Of the other cases, all but one are known to have come before an arbitrator.[8] One case only contains no indication of a public arbitration, but it belongs to the class of cases which were subject to arbitration.[9] These cases then afford no support to the view that documents were filed at the preliminary investigation; for it is admitted that where

[1] D. 45:54; cf. Arist., *Politics*, 1274b, where we have "denunciation" (ἐπίσκηψις) attributed to Charondas as something new; cf. Bentley, *Dissertations*, p. 372.

[2] See Daremberg and Saglio, *Dict. des antiq.*, *s. v.* διαιτηταί.

[3] Arist., *Const. of Athens*, 52:3.

[4] M. S. L., p. 867.

[5] M. S. L., p. 904.

[6] Arist., *Const. of Athens*, 53:2; note p. 190 of Sandys' edition.

[7] D. 45:8, 17, 20, 31, 57; 49:19.

[8] D. 27:51, 54; 28:1; cf. 29:58, which shows that there was a public arbitration; D. 39:17; a comparison of 22 and 37 ff., shows that there was a public arbitration; D. 40:21, 28, 58; cf. 16 and 17 with Sandys' note; D. 47:16; cf. 5; D. 54:27.

[9] D. 48:48; cf. Arist., *Const. of Athens*, 53:2.

arbitration was compulsory, the preliminary investigation was conducted by the arbitrator, and no documents were filed with the magistrate.[1]

The word ἐμβάλλω is so constantly associated with the inclosing of documents in the evidence boxes that it became a technical word for the filing of evidentiary matter, and was so understood without the use of ἐχῖνος.[2] What has usually been regarded as a mere variation is the use of καταβάλλω in Chrysippus v. Phormio.[3] There was no arbitration in this case, which was one of the monthly suits.[4] Is it not possible that the speaker intentionally changed his phraseology to avoid a word which, even when standing alone, would naturally suggest filing with an arbitrator, and used one more appropriate to the action of simply depositing a document with a court official?

Suidas distinguishes two kinds of ἀνάκρισις. The usual form was a simple inquiry into the details of the case, to determine whether under the circumstances an action would lie. If the magistrate decided that he had jurisdiction, and no objection was raised by the defendant, the case went on in the usual way. Ordinarily there was no need of evidence. The pleadings in the case and the answers of the parties themselves would furnish abundant data to enable him to decide the questions that would come up at this stage of the proceedings.[5] If, however, the defendant raised objections and resorted to a special plea (παραγραφή or διαμαρτυρία), the scope of the inquiry was enlarged, and some additional data in the way of the evidence of witnesses might be required.[6] There is nothing, however, in the nature of the proceeding, as set forth by the Orators and lexicographers, to lead one to suppose that the entire body of evidence, or any considerable portion of it, was ever produced at the preliminary investigation.

Isæus presents an instructive picture of the proceedings at an ἀνάκρισις.[7] The object was simply to find out whether the defendant, who had resorted to a διαμαρτυρία, could make out a *prima facie* case. Apparently the statements of the parties, either volunteered or elicited by questions either of the magistrate or of the opponent, backed by the authority of the magistrate,[8] constituted in this case the sole evidence before the court. It is true that the plaintiff demanded that witnesses should be produced, but

1 M. S. L., p. 825. 2 D. 40:21. 3 D. 34:46.

4 Arist., *Const of Athens*, 52 and 59:5.

5 These various questions have been set forth by Caillemer, Daremberg and Saglio, *Dict. des antiq.*, *s. v.*

6 Suidas, *s. v.* ἀνάκρισις and δίκης ἀνάκρισις.

7 Isæ. 6:12 ff. 8 Cf. D. 46:10.

the demand was rejected by the defendants. In fact, the object of the speaker in telling the jury what took place at the preliminary investigation was to show that at that time the defendants failed to produce any evidence to support their case.

A passage in Demosthenes throws some further light on the nature of the preliminary investigation. The plaintiff in Callistratus v. Olympiodorus—a case which arose out of a former suit in which the present parties were codefendants—in giving an account of the earlier litigation, says that after the ἀνάκρισις he and Olympiodorus found themselves totally unprepared to go on with the trial, and cast about for some excuse for delay to enable them to prepare their case.[1] This excuse, however, was not accepted, and the case went against them by default. Now, if all the evidence had been put in at the ἀνάκρισις the preparation of the case for argument would have been a comparatively simple matter. For the plan of defense must have been determined and outlined before the evidence could be arranged and produced. It is inconceivable that a man who had all his documents and affidavits ready, and had the grasp of the case necessary for their preparation, would have risked the loss of his case by trying to have it postponed in order to allow more time for preparation.

An even more convincing instance is afforded by Apollodorus v. Arethusius—a criminal prosecution for false witness to a writ of summons (γραφὴ ψευδοκλητείας). After the preliminary investigation, Apollodorus was assaulted by the defendant one evening as he was returning to the city from the Piræus. A few days afterward the case came up for trial, and this assault was proved to the satisfaction of the jurors, who wished, owing to this and other aggravating circumstances, to inflict the death penalty. It is barely possible that he produced no evidence of this assault; but those who had come to his rescue were available, and without their testimony the jury would scarcely have proposed to inflict so severe a penalty.[2]

Apart from these instances, the Orators pay but slight attention to the proceedings at the preliminary investigation. Little is said about evidence, and we never hear of a witness as being present. Indeed, apart from an ineffectual demand for the production of witnesses, and two challenges to produce slaves, evidence is never mentioned.[3] It is perhaps not a matter of accident that, while the swearing of witnesses is occasionally mentioned in connection with an arbitration, nothing is said of witnesses' oaths at a preliminary hearing.[4] Furthermore, it is remarkable that, while Aristotle

[1] D. 48:23.

[2] D. 53:15–17.

[3] Isæ. 6:15; D. 47:5; 53:22.

[4] D. 45:58; 54:26; cf. Arist. *Const. of Athens*, 55:5.

and the lexicographers all mention written depositions in their discussions of arbitrations, there is nowhere a hint of filing documents at the preliminary hearing. Nor is there in the popular conception of a preliminary hearing any trace of its being connected with the filing of documents. It is regarded as an inquiry conducted by means of question and answer.[1]

The question arises here as to the time when affidavits were filed in cases not subject to arbitration; for they were all in the hands of the clerk on the day of the trial.

Coming to the speeches themselves, we find several instances of evidence being introduced in court that had not been brought out at any previous hearing of the case. Witnesses were frequently unwilling to give evidence, either because they were hostile to, or related to, one or other of the parties, or because they were afraid of exposing themselves to ridicule.[2] In these cases we see that the speaker had no assurance that his witness would accept the deposition. This means, of course, that this evidence had not been produced at any preliminary hearing of the case. It is impossible to say in how many other cases the same thing occurred, for there was no need of mentioning it except when the speaker was not sure of his witness. Reluctant witnesses are called upon for the first time to testify or take an oath of disclaimer in court in two perjury cases;[3] in two cases involving claims to an inheritance;[4] in an appeal from the decision of a deme regarding the status of a citizen;[5] and in four public prosecutions.[6] Now, if these depositions were produced for the first time[7] at the trial, there could have been no arbitration in any of the cases.

But an attempt has been made to reconcile these cases with the supposed rule requiring all evidence to be filed at a preliminary hearing of the case, by assuming that where a witness did not present himself at the preliminary hearing or arbitration for any reason, an affidavit was still put in, though unacknowledged by him.[8] Such depositions could not be used by the presiding official as a basis for his decision and are really not evidence. Not only, however, is there no direct proof of such a practice, but there is actually a case in which it is distinctly stated that an affidavit of an absent witness was not filed before the arbitrator. The plaintiff in Apollodorus v. Timotheus complains that he was unable to put in a certain affidavit

[1] Xen., *Sympos.*, 5:2.

[2] D. 57:14; Isæ. 2:33; Æsch., I, 45 ff.

[3] D. 45:60; Isæ. 2:33. [4] Isæ. 8:42; 9:18. [5] D. 57:14.

[6] D. *De F. L.*, 176; 59:28, 84; 58:7; Æsch. 1:45 ff.

[7] Arist., *Const. of Athens*, 53:2; cf. Hubert, p. 38.

[8] Kennedy in *Dict. of Antiq.*, *s. v.* "Martyria."

in the evidence box, owing to the absence of the witness.[1] Furthermore, indications are not wanting that litigants did not always know just what evidence their opponents would produce. Obviously in these cases the depositions had not been filed at a preliminary hearing.[2]

Our authorities, then, contain no trace of a rule requiring evidence to be filed in writing at the ἀνάκρισις. Indeed, not a few incidents in the speeches can be satisfactorily explained only by supposing that depositions could be deposited with the clerk of the court at any time before they were required to be read.[3]

ARBITRATOR

Before going to law at all, or at any time during the progress of a suit, an agreement to submit differences to private arbitrators was in order.[4] The proceedings were entirely informal. Evidence was not reduced to writing. Women regularly appeared as witnesses. The decision of the arbitrators could be proved by the production of their written award, or by their own evidence before the jury, or by the evidence of anyone who was present at the sessions.[5]

But the majority of private suits were sent to a public arbitrator.[6] The proceedings were less formal than those of a regular court.[7] If a party failed to appear, the decision was given against him. The arbitrator, like the investigating magistrate, conducted the inquiry by means of questions addressed to the parties regarding the details of the case;[8] and we find the parties freely exercising their right to question each other.[9] These cross-examinations often surprised a litigant into making an admission that was afterward used before the jury to his disadvantage, and frequently disclosed many of the arguments he would rely upon in case of an appeal.[10]

Witnesses, upon being summoned, had to appear before the arbitrator.[11] Either party might swear his opponent's witnesses, if he chose.[12] As a

1 D. 49:19 ff.

2 Isæ. 10:23: *ὥστε ἂν ἐπὶ τοῦτον τὸν λόγον καταφεύγῃ καὶ μάρτυρας παρέχηται ὡς διέθετο ἐκεῖνος κ. τ. λ.* Cf. Isæ. 5:4; 6:64; 9:9. These cases are clearly different from those in which a speaker challenges anyone to come forward and give evidence to the contrary, e. g. D. 57:61.

3 Æsch., 1:45, where the language conveys the impression that he produced the document for the first time in the court.

4 Hubert, pp. 8 ff.

5 D. 36:16; 59:71; 43:31; cf. 52:16.

6 Arist., *Const. of Athens*, 53:2.

7 Hubert, p. 43.

8 D. 27:50 ff.

9 D. 49:55; cf. 46:10.

10 D. 49:21, 34; 41:12.

11 D. 29:20; 49:19.

12 D. 45:57; 54:26; cf. p. 76.

rule, the witness was asked to subscribe to an affidavit prepared beforehand.[1] If he refused to subscribe to any particular fact contained in the written deposition, it could be amended to suit him;[2] but if he knew nothing at all about the matter, he could take an oath of disclaimer (ἐξωμοσία), and be relieved from the obligation of attendance in court afterward. Depositions were also prepared at the hearing.[3] This was the regular practice in the case of challenges delivered during a session.[4] If a challenge were accepted, the session could be adjourned to enable the parties to comply with its provisions.[5] An official list of witnesses was probably kept.[6]

Laws, challenges, and documentary evidence of all kinds had to be filed with the arbitrator, and inclosed in the official evidence box of the party who produced them. After these boxes had been sealed, the case was closed, and no further evidence could, as a rule, be introduced in case of an appeal.[7] Along with the pleadings in the case and the evidence, the arbitrator filed his own decision.[8]

Some, relying on a passage in Isæus, have supposed that the arbitrator made a memorandum of the statements and answers of the parties themselves, which was called **ἀπόκρισις**;[9] but an examination of two passages in Demosthenes puts an entirely different complexion upon the passage in Isæus. Demosthenes had an **ἀπόκρισις** of Aphobus read in court, in which he admitted the existence of a will made by the father of Demosthenes, together with the evidence of witnesses who had heard the answers of both Aphobus and his fellow-guardians given either at the **ἀνάκρισις** or at the arbitration.[10] Had the **ἀπόκρισις** been reduced to writing by the magistrate, no verifying witnesses would have been required.[11] In the third speech against Aphobus **ἀπόκρισις** is somewhat loosely used of the evidence of a witness who deposed to an answer of Aphobus before the public arbitrator.[12] To corroborate the witness, Demosthenes had taken the precaution to have a slave on hand to take down the answers of Aphobus.[13] This slave he afterward offered for examination. There can be no doubt that in both cases the answers were taken down at the instance of Demosthenes, and produced by him in court in one case as a separate document verified by evidence, and incorporated with the verifying affidavit in the other.

1 D. 46:11. 2 D. 45:87. 3 D. 29:20; 54:26. 4 D. 46:11; 29:20.
5 D. 54:27. 6 D. 29:15; cf. D. 54:31. 7 D. 39:17.
8 Arist., *Const. of Athens*, 53:2. See p. 55 for full discussion of the exceptions.
9 M. S. L., p. 903; Platner, Vol. I, p. 133; Scheibe, *Isæus*, Index, *s. v.* ἀπόκρισις.
10 D. 27:42; cf. Kennedy's note, Dem. V: 103.
11 D. 27:41. 12 D. 29:10, 31, 59. 13 D. 29:11.

CHAPTER IX

EVIDENCE IN COURT

The method of presenting evidence to the jury was determined largely by rhetorical considerations.[1] The affidavits and other documents were read by the clerk of the court when called for. On one occasion the speaker, after calling for a document, remarks: "Look carefully. It ought to be there somewhere;" and while the clerk is looking for it, he continues his speech.[2] This may have been a device arranged in advance to give the impression that the further eulogy bestowed upon Chabrias was extemporaneous. Lysias excuses the introduction of witnesses who, in view of the jury's complete knowledge of the subject, might be deemed unnecessary, by saying that he needed a rest.[3] Evidence was sometimes introduced without any mention being made of it in the speech.[4] On the other hand, at times not all the evidence that was prepared was read in court.[5] Demosthenes in his speech against Meidias[6] called for the first affidavit of a witness; but there is no mention of the second. It may have been omitted altogether, or introduced without specific mention. Documents were sometimes read in sections with a running commentary,[7] or the whole document was repeated later in the same speech.[8] Demosthenes has the entire evidence read again in the second speech against Aphobus.[9] In Androcles v. Lacritus depositions are read which were drawn up with a view to a lawsuit against another person connected with the same subject-matter.[10] And evidence used in one case may be produced in another.[11] A summary of the evidence to be given may precede the reading of the deposition, or the chief points may be indicated after the reading;[12] but the general practice was to introduce the reading of evidence with some brief remark, such as: "I shall produce evidence of these matters;" "To show that I am telling the truth, read the evidence;" "Call me witnesses of these things." A perusal of a speech will indicate pretty accurately the nature of the evidence offered, if not the actual contents of the affidavits, as is shown by the numerous forgeries of affidavits scattered throughout the speeches of Demosthenes, the contents of which

[1] See Léon Moy, *Étude sur les plaidoyers d'Isée*, pp. 54 ff.

[2] D. 20:84. [3] Lys. 12:61.

[4] Blass, III, l. 232; Guggenheim, p. 41. [5] D. 42:26.

[6] D. 21:21. [7] D. 45:25; And. 1:47. [8] D. 35:37. [9] D. 28:11 ff.

[10] D. 35:20; Blass, III, l. 563, n. 2. [11] Isæ. 3:7, 11.

[12] D. 44:44; Lys. 31:14; Isæ. 1:15; D. 37:9.

can in many cases be shown to have been drawn from the speech itself.[1] Nevertheless, they have some value as indicating what later writers supposed the usual form of such affidavits to be; and the well-known persistence of legal forms makes it almost certain that the forms are substantially the same as those used in the time of the Orators.

Several affidavits have been preserved in the body[2] of a speech to which the spurious depositions bear a more or less close resemblance. The usual affidavit was a mere statement that the witness was cognizant of a single definite fact; but, if we may judge by the forgeries, many were comparatively diffuse. The names of plaintiff and defendant were recited, and the means the witnesses had for knowing about the transactions in question, such as his relationship to the party for whom the testimony is given, or his presence at the transaction.

A number of witnesses frequently subscribed to the same affidavit. A deposition was usually confined to a single fact, and so one witness might be called upon to make more than one deposition in the same case.[3] When a deposition was read, the witness was required to go forward and acknowledge it as his own.[4]

The rule that forbade the production of documents or depositions after the case was closed by the arbitrator could be waived by consent of the parties. A common example is a challenge to produce a slave or a document.[5] If the challenge was accepted, the evidence was admissible. Another instance of the waiving of the rule is where the speaker, in order to make his statements more impressive, challenges anyone to come forward and give evidence to the contrary.[6]

It is obvious also that the court had power to authorize the introduction of new evidence.[7] Evidence respecting events that occurred subsequently to the arbitration could probably not be produced except by consent of one's opponents or by permission of the courts;[8] but nothing prevented the speaker from adverting to such matters.[9]

A question arises in respect to the proceedings before the arbitrator. The plaintiff in Ariston v. Conon brings witnesses to show that Conon's conduct at the arbitration was vexatious; and evidence is also brought to

[1] For the literature on this subject see Blass, III, l. 467.

[2] D. 29:31; 54:31.

[3] D. 54:10, 12.

[4] D. 47:3; Isoc. 17:14. An exception was allowed when the witness was ill or abroad; see p. 25.

[5] D. 47:16; 48:50.

[6] Cf. Lys. 20:11; D. 57:61.

[7] Æsch. 2:126; D. 57:65, 67.

[8] D. 39:17.

[9] D. 39:37, 38.

establish the answers of the parties before the arbitrator.[1] As the arbitrator himself was aware of these matters there was no need of evidence regarding them to be produced at the arbitration. Such testimony was in all probability exempt from the rule limiting the evidence to the documents filed with the arbitrator.

The case of the witness Antiphanes, mentioned in Apollodorus v. Timotheus, presents some difficulty. He had failed to appear at the arbitration. Consequently, the plaintiff was unable to file his evidence. Both a suit for failure to testify and a suit for damages were instituted. When the original case came up for trial, the plaintiff proposed to call Antiphanes to give evidence.[2] If, as Rentzsch[3] believes, he gave evidence, we must suppose that the fact that legal proceedings had been instituted against the witness enabled the plaintiff to introduce the evidence, although it had not been previously filed. But no rule can be confidently deduced from the passage.

Down to the time of Isæus, as we have seen, oral evidence was the rule. Andocides, however, not only introduces oral evidence, but actually elicits it by question and answer in the case of one witness.[4] Volkmann compares this with the practice of addressing questions to an opponent in court;[5] but the practice is rather the outcome of the regular oral evidence than the extension of the public examination of an opponent. Diffuseness and lack of definiteness are apt to characterize the evidence of one who is allowed to tell his own story. It is not surprising that Andocides seized upon the only means of correcting this defect. The wonder is that the practice did not become general.

Another kind of oral evidence recognized by law consists of the answers of a suitor to the questions of an opponent. The law required that all these questions be answered.[6] This, of course, has reference to the regular judicial hearings of a case, preliminary investigation,[7] arbitration,[8] and trial. Where a party to a suit was surprised into a damaging admission in the presence of his opponent, or of someone friendly to him outside of the court, it was the regular practice to have witnesses testify to these

[1] D. 29:10; 49:34.

[2] D. 49:20: *ἀξιῶ αὐτὸν ἀναβάντα εἰπεῖν ἐναντίον ὑμῶν διομοσάμενον πρῶτον μὲν εἰ ἐδάνεισεν Τιμοθέῳ χιλίας δραχμάς, δεύτερον δ' εἰ παρὰ τοῦ πατρὸς Φίλιππος ἀπέλαβε τοῦτο τὸ ἀργύριον.*

[3] Rentzsch, p. 24. There is no indication that the witness did testify, and the word ἀξιῶ suggests a challenge quite as much as a demand (cf. D. 48:48, 50).

[4] And. 1:14.

[5] Volkmann, *Rhet.*, p. 189. [6] D. 46:10. [7] Cf. p. 49. [8] Cf. p. 52.

admissions, though the evidence was really hearsay.[1] But there was no provision for the examination of an opponent on certain specific points, such as is known in English law as examination for discovery. There was, indeed, no need of such a provision, as any question could be put at the preliminary investigation or arbitration; and the magistrate had the power of insisting upon an answer.[2] At the trial he could not be a witness in his own behalf, except in so far as his speech could be considered evidence. But when questioned in court he virtually became a witness for his opponent. Technically, however, his answers were not evidence, nor was he, so far as we know, liable for perjury.

Lysias is the only orator who availed himself of the privilege of questioning his opponent before the jury. He questions Eratosthenes, whom he was prosecuting for the murder of his brother. He first apologizes for speaking to such a man, and abruptly orders him to come forward: "Come up here and answer my questions."[3] And so in the other cases he speaks as if he were availing himself of an indisputable right. The answers are always admissions, which in two cases are coupled with an excuse.[4] Several examples of imaginary questions and dialogues with opponents occur in other orators, and some are quite effective as rhetorical devices.[5] Andocides introduces a supposititious case, in which he pictures himself as being examined by one of the Thirty.[6] So Plato represents Socrates as questioning Meletus.[7] Perhaps the most effective interrogation is found in Deinarchus.[8] Lysias makes particularly good use of the admission of the corn-dealers by treating it as a confession and demanding a conviction.

We can only conjecture why the practice fell into disuse after the time of Lysias. Possibly the disadvantages attending it outweighed any advantage to be gained from it. The admissions could be secured more safely at the preliminary examination, for there was always the danger that the opponent would boldly resort to falsehood. This would be a serious rebuff, even if it could easily be shown that the answers were not true. Lysias suggests this possibility, and cleverly guards against it by saying: "I don't fancy you will deny what you did in presence of all the Athenians."[9]

[1] Cf. p. 24. [2] Isæ. 6:12. [3] Lys. 12:24.

[4] Lys. 12:25; he acknowledges the murder, but claims he was obliged to do it. Lys. 22:5; the excuse for breaking the law is the orders of grain inspectors.

[5] D. 29:41: "Which of the witnesses did you prosecute for perjury? Tell me. But you can't"; 39:30; 37:57; Isæ. 11:5.

[6] And. 1:101. [7] Plato, *Apol.*, 24 D.

[8] Dein. 1:83. Cf. Volkmann, pp. 189, 190. [9] Lys. 13:32.

And Demosthenes on one occasion says: "I would gladly question Theocrines, if he would answer me truly."[1] However successful the examination was, nothing was proved that could not otherwise be proved.[2]

It will be convenient to mention at this point the matter of cross-examination of witnesses, though neither Lysias' questions to his opponents nor Andocides' examination of the witness are instances of cross-examination. Cross-examination in English law is used of the questions put to the witnesses on the other side, confined to matters dealt with in the examination in chief. Of this most effective method of confounding the witnesses of an adversary Greek practice knows nothing. There was an opportunity for it at the arbitration, or at the preliminary examination if the witness was present. But as no reference to it occurs, we may conclude that it was not customary to question an opponent's witness.

The questions which a juryman was allowed to address to the litigants might approximate very closely a regular cross-examination. Not only do the speakers ask the jury to indicate whether the explanations regarding a certain point have been sufficient,[3] and offer to call more advocates if they desire it,[4] but they are ever ready to suggest telling questions to be put to their opponents by the jury.[5] It is impossible to determine to what extent they availed themselves of their privilege of putting questions to the litigants, or how effective their questions were in exposing falsehood or forcing admissions. Neither do we know whether the jurymen stood up and asked their questions, as Andocides suggests,[6] or interrupted the speaker unceremoniously, as Demosthenes bids them do.[7] But whether the questions took the form of a cross-examination or were mere interruptions, they constituted a danger against which a speaker must be prepared. There was, however, so far as we know, no legal obligation to answer these questions,[8] but few would have the hardihood to refuse.

CHAPTER X

PROOF OF LAWS, OFFICIAL RECORDS, AND PRIVATE DOCUMENTS

LAWS

It is misleading to say that, if a speaker wished to use a law before the court, he had to make a copy and have it read by the clerk.[9] Antiphon nowhere has an extract from a law read; he either assumes a knowledge

[1] D. 58:45; cf. 39:30.
[2] Lys. 13:32.
[3] And. 1:33.
[4] D. 34:52.
[5] D. 35:43; 36:34.
[6] And. 1:70; cf. D. 40:54.
[7] D. 41:17; 43:33.
[8] Cf. D. 40:47.
[9] M. S. L., p. 867.

of the law,[1] or refers in a very general way to some of its provisions.[2] Andocides usually has the clerk read the laws, but he sometimes follows the practice of Antiphon.[3] As a rule, the source of the law is not indicated.[4] It probably seemed needless to cite authority for laws which were accessible to all.[5] This was particularly the case after the revision of the laws on the restoration of the democracy in 403 B. C. The revised laws were for the most part posted on the walls of the στοὰ βασίλειος, where anyone who wished could read them.[6] Those that referred to murder were set up on the Areopagus.[7] Some were never set up anywhere, but kept in the Metroon.[8]

Only written laws could be cited after 403.[9] "The unwritten laws in accordance with which the Eumolpidæ expounded" constituted an exception; but it seems that the Eumolpidæ alone had the privilege of expounding[10] them. Neither does this provision apply to the unwritten laws discussed by Aristotle.[11] No mention is made of procuring official copies of laws. When Lysias says that Nicomachus[12] doled out laws to contending parties like a steward, he must be understood as speaking of an exceptional circumstance. The penalty for citing a law that did not exist was death.[13]

In quoting laws, even when the exact words are purported to be given, it is probable that the speaker allowed himself considerable latitude in the way of omissions and transpositions; it was sufficient if the quotation was not materially different from the original law. A comparison of the law of Dracon respecting murder, cited by Demosthenes in the speech against Macartatus, with the original law, as deciphered by Köhler in 1867, shows that Demosthenes took considerable liberty with the text in order to group together those parts of the law that were calculated to elucidate the point he was arguing.[14] While the comparison establishes beyond reasonable doubt the authenticity of this particular law, it goes a long way to confirm confidence in the genuineness of other laws quoted in the manuscripts of the different speeches.[15]

1 Ant. 5:9; 1:29. 2 Ant. 5:12, 48. 3 And. 1:95.

4 D. 35:51; 36:24 ff.; 38:17; Lys. 10:14; Isæ. 3:38; but cf. And. 1:95; Lys. 6:15; D. 20:128; 58:56; 59:76.

5 D. 20:93; 47:71. 6 And. 1:83 ff.

7 D. 47:71; Lys. 6:15. 8 M. S. L., p. 868. 9 And. 1:85.

10 Lys. 6:9; And. 1:115, 116, with Marchand's note.

11 Arist., *Rhet.*, 1:15, 3 ff. 12 Lys. 30:3. 13 D. 26:24; cf. M. S. L., p. 867.

14 Köhler, *Hermes*, II (1867), p. 27. Dittenberger, *Sylloge*², No. 52.

15 Cf. Dareste, *Les plaidoyers civils de Demosthène*, Vol. II, p. 26; cf. Barrilleau, *Des sources du droit grec*, p. 8.

COURT RECORDS

Pleadings of former legal proceedings are read in court without any attempt to establish their authenticity. There is no indication that they had an official source,[1] though we are told that the indictment of Socrates was preserved in the Metroon.[2] Each party to the suit had copies of the pleadings of his opponents, which must have been obtained originally from the office of the magistrate before whom the suit began. Thus in a subsequent suit between the same parties or their heirs[3] these pleadings could be produced without application to a magistrate. The risk of prompt exposure of anything in the nature of a forgery would be so great as to insure that the pleadings cited would be correct. It was not the practice to make use of judicial records, and there is reason to doubt if there were any adequate means for recording the verdicts of the courts. Where, however, a man was condemned to pay a fine to the state, his name was registered as a public debtor.[4] Andocides has the clerk read a list of those who were condemned in connection with the profanation of the Mysteries and the mutilation of the Hermæ. These lists are verified in one case by the evidence of one who was officially connected with the investigation; in another, by an appeal to the knowledge of the jury; in a third, by a challenge to any one of the persons so condemned to come forward and disprove his statements.[5] In fact, if there were complete official records, the charge that Andocides was himself an informer could have been definitely established or refuted by a simple reference to the records. Lysias gives a similar list.[6] The previous examination of Agoratus may have established its correctness. Thus, in proving anything connected with judicial proceedings, persons who were present could testify,[7] or the officials themselves could be summoned,[8] or an appeal to the knowledge of the jury could be made.[9] Reference is occasionally made to the failure of a litigant to get a fifth part of the votes. This would be indicated by the judgment. The exact number of votes by which a party gained or lost a suit is occasionally given. There is nothing to lead us to suppose that there was an official source for the information, but as the result of the vote was always announced by the herald, it was known to a large number of people.[10]

[1] D. 38:15; 34:16, 17; cf. Volkmann, pp. 180 ff.

[2] Favorinus in *Frag. hist. Graec.*, Vol. III, p. 578, 5; cf. Schanz, Plato's *Apol.*, pp. 12 ff.

[3] D. 38:15. [4] D. 58:50. [5] And. 1:13 ff., 35. [6] Lys. 13:38.

[7] Lys. 23:14; D. 53:18; 30:32.

[8] Lys. 17:8. [9] Ant. 6:38.

[10] Isæ. 3:37; D. 21:75; Arist. *Const. of Athens*, col. 35, ll. 31 ff.

OFFICIAL REGISTERS

Official registers could probably be produced in court. Demosthenes, in giving a rough estimate of the amount of grain imported from the Pon us, says that the exact amount could be ascertained by an inspection of the register of the corn-inspectors.[1] In Chrysippus v. Phormio he makes use of the books of the customs officers, but his language leaves it uncertain whether the register itself was produced, or simply an extract with a deposition showing that it was correct.[2] Lysias attacks the official cavalry register of the Thirty as inaccurate, and claims that a list in the hands of the phylarchs is more accurate. Witnesses are brought to prove that the name of Mantitheus is not in the latter list.[3] As the evidence from these lists was negative, an extract would not serve the purpose. In a claim against the state for confiscated property of one indebted to the defendant, the official schedules of the property are read in court.[4]

It would seem that there was no settled practice in regard to official papers. If the originals could not conveniently be produced, copies or extracts, verified possibly by the evidence of the officials, were employed. The evidence of persons who had inspected them was also allowed.[5]

PROVING THE EXECUTION AND CONTENTS OF PRIVATE DOCUMENTS

Private documents, as distinguished from official documents and court records, comprised among others, contracts, wills, account-books, and letters.[6] These are not to be confused with matters which were reduced to writing in order to be read in court, such as laws, oaths, oracles, challenges, and lists of liturgies.[7] There is no apparent uniformity in the means employed in proving the contents of a document. Sometimes the original instrument was produced. This was the usual practice where it was desired to prove the contents of a will. Occasional instances are found where the evidence of the depositee alone was deemed sufficient to prove the authenticity of the will produced;[8] and very frequently no better evidence was forthcoming, as testators did not always read the contents of the will to the witnesses.[9] Thus the evidence of the ordinary witness

[1] D. 20:39.

[2] D. 34:7: λαβὲ δὴ καὶ τὴν τῶν πεντηκοστολόγων ἀπογραφὴν καὶ τὰς μαρτυρίας; cf. D. 58:8.

[3] Lys. 16:6 ff.

[4] Lys. 17:4, 9.

[5] Modern practice in proving official documents is largely regulated by statute law.

[6] Isoc. 17:52; D., *De Cor.*, 39, 78; Lys. 20:27; D. 59:78; 48:48; 36:19 ff.

[7] Lys. 19:57; D. 30:36; 22:23; 21:130.

[8] D. 45:17; Isæ. 9:24.

[9] Isæ. 4:12 ff.

could prove nothing beyond the fact that a will had been made. Nevertheless, several of the wills that are met with in the Orators were accompanied by the evidence of the witnesses alone, unless the depositee was treated as a witness.[1] Wills that were sealed afforded exceptional opportunities for establishing their genuineness. Seals might be affixed either by the testator himself or by his executor after his decease.[2]

Only one case is found where a copy of the will was submitted to the jury. Phormio offered a copy, rather than the original, for the purpose of entrapping the plaintiff, Apollodorus, into acknowledging as his father's will a document which, he maintained, was a forgery. Possibly the defendant resorted to this challenge because, owing to the death of the original depositee, he would have had difficulty in establishing the genuineness of the document, which he claimed was the will.[3] Provisions in wills were proved also by the evidence of those who knew the contents.[4] There is abundant evidence that it was comparatively easy to have a false will accepted as genuine.[5]

As in the case of wills, so in the case of other documents, various ways of proving the contents were adopted. Examples occur where the document is accompanied by the evidence of both witnesses and depositee.[6] But less elaborate proof was usually deemed sufficient. No great importance was attached to the production of the original document, as is seen in the case of Callistratus v. Olympiodorus, where the plaintiff challenged his opponent to have copies of the contract submitted to the court. He might as well have insisted on the production of the original.[7] As the challenge was refused, Callistratus, in order to prove the terms of the contract, was obliged to resort to other means, consisting of his own statements and the evidence of the depositee.[8]

Nor was the use of this and similar kinds of secondary evidence exceptional, although its obvious unfairness under certain circumstances has not escaped notice. The law, it is true, nowhere made any regulations regarding the use of secondary evidence of documents, but Demosthenes suggests a limitation which may well have found favor in the eyes of the jury, owing to its evident fairness. The facts of the case are briefly these: Two for-

[1] Isæ. 3:56; 6:7; cf. 9:12.

[2] D. 28:5; 45:17.

[3] D. 36:7; 45:17 ff.

[4] D. 27:42; 41:6, 17 ff.

[5] Isæ. 5:6 ff., where the same person claimed under two different wills, both of which were proved to be false.

[6] D. 35:10 ff.

[7] D. 48:48.

[8] D. 48:11; cf. Isæ. 5:2, 25, where a contract, partly written and partly oral, was proved by depositions.

eigners, Parmeno and Apaturius, had agreed to refer certain matters in dispute between them to arbitration. During the sittings of the arbitrators a dispute as to the terms of the reference arose. Parmeno called for the contract. The depositee appeared and asserted that it was lost. In spite of Parmeno's protest against Apaturius' interpretation of the contract, the decision was given against him. Apaturius now proceeded against the plaintiff in the present suit, as surety of Parmeno, to recover the amount of the award. The plaintiff denied that he was named in the contract as surety, and entered a special plea on the ground that there was no contract between them. But the defendant, though relying entirely upon the contract between himself and Parmeno, did not produce it. To prove its terms, he relied upon his own assertions[1] and upon the evidence of the depositee of the contract.[2] The gist of the argument on this point was that, since the articles of agreement, which were constructively in the possession of Apaturius, and certainly beyond the control of the plaintiff, had been lost, or rather suppressed, by the defendant in collusion with the depositee, he ought not to be allowed to give secondary evidence of the contents.[3] Unfortunately, we do not know the result of the suit. We can only conjecture that a litigant who appealed to a document which he had wrongfully suppressed laid himself open to a telling attack and materially lessened his chances of success.

The purport of the evidence of a depositee in connection with the production of what appears to be an original document is worthy of notice. In Androcles v. Lacritus,[4] the actual affidavit is inserted. The chief point in the deposition is that the document is still in possession of the depositee. The question of the genuineness of this document need not trouble us here, though the balance of opinion is in favor of its authenticity,[5] since we can glean from the text of another speech that evidence to the same effect was submitted to the jury.[6] One can see how such evidence could be given at the arbitration, where the document was handed over to be put on file, but it was far from the truth at the time of a subsequent trial. Perhaps the most natural explanation of this anomaly is to assume that it was understood that the evidence referred to the time of arbitration and not to the time of the trial. It is just possible, however, that in these cases an admitted copy was introduced by the co-operation of both parties, both of whom would in most cases desire to have the instrument before the court. This would explain why Callistratus in the first instance asked for a copy rather than the original.[7]

[1] D. 33:35 ff. [2] D. 33:38. [3] D. 33:37–8. [4] D. 35:14.
[5] See Sandys' note on the passage. [6] D. 41:8–10, 21. [7] D. 48:48.

Considering, then, the small importance attached to the production of original documents, we are not surprised to find that scarcely any provision was made for securing documentary evidence by process of law. If a document belonged absolutely to a man, he could secure it from the bailee, whether he was a regular depositee or one who had improperly secured possession of it, by summoning him to produce it at a certain time and place. If the demand were refused, resort could be had to a δίκη εἰς ἐμφανῶν κατάστασιν.[1] There is no instance of evidentiary matter being recovered in this way, though we can see no reason why recourse was not had to this means in a case in Lysias. The guardian, Diogeiton, had through false pretenses secured from the widow of the testator a duplicate copy of the will under which he acted. The document would have been of great service in establishing the amount of property claimed by the wards, and yet there was no attempt made to regain possession of it.[2]

As to the means at the disposal of a ward who desired to compel the production of a will in the hands of his guardians, our authorities leave us in considerable doubt. Demosthenes asserts that, if the will came into the hands of the executors, it was their duty to seal it in presence of the witnesses, that it might be preserved intact and be available in case of dispute; but, if the will was already in the custody of a depositee, they were to call upon him to produce it in any subsequent litigation. It is significant, however, that in neither of these suits was the actual will produced. A copy was offered in one case, and some business papers in the other.[3] How far the guardians' action in these cases could be construed into a compliance with the law it is difficult to decide. For in neither case did the plaintiff go beyond a protest. Taking these cases together with the Diogeiton case in Lysias, already mentioned,[4] we may assume that the guardian could not be compelled to produce a will. On the distribution of the property the business papers of the deceased went to the heirs.[5] Where the heirs were adults, and there were no guardians, the usual practice was to seal up and deposit all papers connected with the disposition of the property after making copies of them.[6]

Documentary evidence in the hands of an opponent could not be secured except by his consent. The only course to follow was to challenge him to produce it for inspection and copying.[7]

[1] Isæ. 6:31; M. S. L., p. 871.

[2] Lys. 32:7.

[3] D. 28:5 ff.; 45:17.

[4] Lys. 32:7.

[5] D. 36:20; 49:43.

[6] D. 41:21.

[7] D. 49:43, where the bank ledgers are produced according to a challenge delivered at the arbitration.

Contracts present a peculiar feature, which merits a detailed statement. Platner states very explicitly that either party to a contract could use it as evidence, even against the will of the other party.[1] In proof he cites a statement of Demosthenes that contracts are sealed and deposited with trustworthy persons *ἵν', ἐάν τι ἀντιλέγωσιν, ᾖ αὐτοῖς ἐπανελθοῦσιν ἐπὶ τὰ γράμματα, ἐντεῦθεν τὸν ἔλεγχον ποιήσασθαι περὶ τοῦ ἀμφισβητουμένου.*[2] But he has missed the point in the passage, which is the very opposite of his contention. Clearly the inspection is to be made by both parties together.[3] The object in depositing a contract was not merely for safekeeping, but rather to prevent substitutions and changes by the parties themselves. And there is plenty of proof that it was not a useless precaution.[4] If for any purpose an inspection was desired, a summons had to be issued to the depositee to appear with the document on a specified day at a certain place, where both parties would be present. It was customary for the contracting parties to keep copies of contracts for their own private purposes, to remind them of their rights and obligations in the matter.[5]

The leading case on the production of a contract is Callistratus v. Olympiodorus, where an unsuccessful effort was made to have the defendant consent to the production either of the original contract or of a copy. Early in the case the plaintiff had issued a challenge to join in making copies and inclosing them in the evidence boxes. The defendant, who pleaded that, owing to the default of the other contracting party, he was no longer bound by its terms, refused, in order that the jury might not hear the document from admitted copies.[6] It by no means follows, as Platner[7] holds, that acceptance of the challenge by Olympiodorus would have carried with it an admission that the contract was binding. His defense, based on the alleged default of Callistratus, would still have been available. Nothing would be admitted beyond the genuineness of the copy. At the trial the challenge was renewed; but this time it involved the reading of

1 Platner, Vol. I, p. 254.

2 D. 33:36.

3 Cf. Beauchet, Vol. IV, p. 62; Heffter, p. 303.

4 Isoc. 17:23; D. 33:17 ff.

5 Cf. D. 37:42, where a contracting party neglected, to his cost, to take a copy of the contract. And so in the *Athenogenes* of Hyperides (10), when the plaintiff found that he had been deceived regarding the transaction involving the purchase of a slave, he summoned his friends and read a copy of the contract to them.

6 D. 48:49.

7 Platner, Vol. I, p. 254.

the original document to the jury.[1] To facilitate the carrying out of this proposal, the depositee had been summoned to court with the contract, and had already appeared as a witness.[2] His evidence was intended to show that the document was in his possession continuously from the time of the deposit.[3] As he was also a witness to the contract, he may have testified to its terms. Nothing in the language of the second challenge suggests that acquiescence on the part of the defendant would have implied any admission on his part regarding the validity and binding effect of the contract. The sole ground of his refusal, according to the speaker, was his unwillingness to have the jury hear the terms of the contract. So far as we can see, Callistratus could not himself order the reading of the document in court. Why should a man who was suing on a contract forego the benefit of having it read in court for the mere purpose of exposing his opponent to the possible disadvantages resulting from the refusal of the challenge? And, besides, when the plaintiff was assured before trial of the determination of his opponent to refuse to sanction the production of the contract, why did he not himself produce it and reap the obvious advantage of having it before the jury? He would still have been able to throw discredit on his opponent by showing his unwillingness to have the jury hear the contract. Now, from the standpoint of the depositee, there was ample ground for his refusal to give up a document without the consent of both parties, even if it were to be in the custody of an official;[4] for he was liable to an action for damages in case of the loss of the document.[5] Callistratus was in both cases careful to mention his willingness to have the contract resealed and deposited. This serves to show how all-important it was that no opportunity should be allowed for tampering with a contract. If however the depositee chose to take the risk of producing the contract with the consent of one part only, there is no indication that the other party could prevent him.

An appeal to the other cases in which contracts were introduced gives no support to Platner's contention. For there is no single case in which it can be shown both that the original document was produced and that the other party had refused to consent to the production.

[1] D. 48:50.

[2] D. 48:11.

[3] Cf. D. 35:14, where a depositee's evidence to this effect is inserted.

[4] Cf. D. 45:57, where the theft of a filed document is mentioned.

[5] D. 33:17, 38.

CHAPTER XI

CHALLENGES

Pollux defines a challenge as an offer or demand to decide the matter in dispute according to an oath, deposition, examination of a slave, or some similar means.[1] It is of the essence of a challenge that the parties abide by the result of the test. We find challenges to refer a dispute to arbitration;[2] to produce documents;[3] to acknowledge a document as a true copy of a will;[4] to leave a certain point or the whole case to the evidence of a particular witness or to the answers of a slave;[5] to produce or accept slaves for torture;[6] to give or accept an oath;[7] or to go outside of Attica to ascertain the truth of a foreign transaction.[8]

The challenges that appear in Antiphon are less formal than the regular challenges of later times, which were usually reduced to writing. In the trial of the stepmother he did not even take the pains to produce proof that the challenge was really delivered, trusting evidently that his opponents would not venture to deny it.[9] In a later case he mentions, without proof, an oral challenge which was made in a courtroom in the presence of jurors and spectators.[10] The best practice was to have the challenge reduced to writing and proved by the deposition of the witnesses who were present;[11] but it was not unusual to combine the two.[12] A challenge could be given at any time between the institution of a suit and a judgment, or even before the institution of a suit.[13] If it was accepted, it was reduced to writing[14] in the form of a sealed and signed contract with sureties for its performance.[15] If refused it was included among the other documents in the case[16] or proved by witnesses. Challenges, according to Demosthenes, were devised for

1 Pollux, VIII, 62; cf. Harpocration. *s. v.* πρόκλησις; Volkmann, pp. 178 ff.

2 D. 40:44; 52:14, 30.

3 D. 27:40; 48:49; cf. p. 64.

4 D. 45:24 ff.

5 Ant. 6:23; Lyc. 1:28.

6 And. 1:9; Lys. 7:34; Isæ. 6:16.

7 D. 29:26, 51; 33:13; Isæ. 12:9.

8 D. 45:16; 32:18.

9 Ant. 1:6 ff.

10 Ant. 6:24.

11 D. 59:123.

12 D. 45:8; cf. Guggenheim, p. 38, whose treatment of the whole subject is very complete.

13 D. 34:28; 48:50; cf. Ant. 6:21.

14 The challenge when given might be either oral or written; D. 37:40; cf. D. 46:11 with Guggenheim's remarks, p. 42.

15 D. 37:40 ff.; cf. M. S. L., p. 891; Guggenheim, p. 42.

16 D. 47:16.

those transactions which could not actually be brought before the jury. He gives as example the torture of a slave, which could not take place in court; and any transaction that took place outside of Attica.[1]

Challenges are not included by Aristotle among πίστεις ἄτεχνοι. It would seem that they ought to be included among the means by which statements are corroborated, and it has been proposed to add a sixth to Aristotle's five classes.[2] The evidentiary value is inferior to that of a document or deposition; for the refusal of a challenge is not direct evidence. A deduction must be made from the facts set forth; and the inference that the refusal arose from a consciousness of guilt is not always correct. For example, the person demanded may not be a slave, but a freedman. Following Demosthenes, Isocrates, and Isæus, who call a challenge τεκμήριον, we may call challenges inferential evidence.[3]

Considerable stress is laid upon the evidentiary value of a challenge. In Apollodorus v. Stephanus the plaintiff promises to produce a challenge by which the jury will catch these men in the act of swearing falsely. And when he produces it, he says: "Take and read this deposition and challenge, in order that they may be forthwith convicted of swearing a false oath."[4] A comparison of two passages in Demosthenes will illustrate the real value of an ordinary challenge as corroborative inferential evidence. In two different speeches he cites his mother as authority for two statements. The first related to the contents of his father's will; the second, to a transaction that took place at the time of his father's death. In the second speech he not only cites his mother as his authority, but challenges his opponent to accept her oath. No one can doubt that this statement, corroborated by the rejected challenge, was more impressive and convincing than the first.[5] Whatever value such corroboration might have, it was always sufficient to free a speaker from the reproach of having asked the jury to believe his bare word. If he had demanded his opponent to produce a slave or a document, he could, on the rejection of a demand, proceed to place before the court what he could have proved conclusively by these means. His opponent could not object to the sufficiency of the corroborative evidence without giving a good reason for his refusal to produce the slave or document.

The burden of proof was often shifted in this way and the opponent put on his defense.[6] But the explanation of the reason for the refusal did not always involve a disadvantage. The plaintiff in Apollodorus v.

[1] D. 45:15 ff.

[2] Volkmann, p. 178.

[3] Isoc. 17:53; D. 40:44; Isæ. 8:6.

[4] D. 45:59, 61.

[5] D. 27:40; 29:26.

[6] Lys. 4:10, 18; D. 48:48 ff.

Timotheus had refused to accept his opponent's oath, and seized the occasion to score him severely as being utterly untrustworthy, by recalling instances of his well-known disregard for an oath.[1] A counter challenge was a favorite means of neutralizing the effect of a refusal to accept a challenge.[2] According to the plaintiff in Ariston v. Conon, a challenge was sometimes given for the purpose of vexatiously delaying a suit.[3]

CHAPTER XII

EVIDENCE OF SLAVES

The evidence of a slave was not accepted in Athenian courts, unless it was taken under torture. The state had the power to torture the slaves of private individuals to secure evidence against their masters. This power was exercised only on rare occasions.[4] But slaves suspected of crime were regularly tortured to secure a confession. Neither sex nor tender years protected the unfortunate slave.[5] Parties to a suit could not secure the evidence of slaves belonging to a third party without his consent;[6] and public slaves were not available as witnesses except with the consent of the magistrates.[7] One of two joint owners of a slave could not without the consent of his partner examine him to secure evidence in his favor regarding a matter in dispute between them, even when the slave was in his possession.[8]

An apparent exception occurs where, on the division of an estate, the heirs agreed to reserve the slaves as common property, to enable either party to obtain by torture or otherwise any property which they suspected that the slaves were concealing.[9] But even if, as some[10] hold, it was intended that these slaves might be tortured by either of the owners to secure evidence to be used in furthering additional claims to the estate, it was nevertheless a special privilege secured by the agreement, and furnishes no ground for regarding the exercise of such a privilege as an incident of ordinary joint ownership.

[1] D. 49:65. [2] Guggenheim, p. 55. [3] D. 54:27.

[4] And. I, 22, 64; cf. Mahaffy, *Social Life in Greece*, p. 241.

[5] Ant. 1:20; 5:69.

[6] Ant. 6:23.

[7] D. 53:23, 25.

[8] Lys. 4:13.

[9] D. 40:15; cf. D. 48:14–18, where the heirs actually did recover property secreted by a slave who had belonged to the deceased; cf. Guggenheim, p. 29.

[10] See Sandys' note on the passage.

The recognized method of making use of the knowledge of one's own slave was to offer him to the other side to be examined under torture. If the challenge was not accepted, the refusal could be used in argument with considerable effect; but a master might torture his slaves to secure a confession for his own private purposes.[1] There was nothing to prevent a speaker's using in his speech information extorted in this way.[2] Under these circumstances, however, the confession or answers of the slave do not constitute evidence. The statement of Athenian practice on this point contained in the first edition of *Der attische Process*—viz., "Die peinliche Befragung wurde nicht anders als auf eine deshalb an den Gegner erlassene Provocation angestellt"—seems to be the correct view. Guggenheim[3] quotes it with approval, but after a discussion of three cases he reaches the conclusion: "Erst nach Anhebung der formellen Klage war Folterung ohne Provocation unzulässig."[4] Lipsius accepts this conclusion in his revision of *Der attische Process*.[5] Apparently this view of Guggenheim results from a confusion between a slave witness and an informer.

The case from Demosthenes[6] merely establishes the fact, as already pointed out, that a master could extract information from a slave by any means he saw fit to use. It is true that a slave might implicate another as an accomplice; or a master might, as in the Lysias case,[7] on suspecting that a slave knew of a crime or wrong being done him, extort information that would lead to the discovery of the culprit. But there is nothing in the case to indicate that the slave girl's answers, had they been extorted by torture and not by threats, could have been used as evidence in any legal proceedings. The use that he does make of her confession, when tried for the murder of Eratosthenes, by no means permits it to be regarded as evidence. Had he wished to use the servant's answers, he would have been obliged to proceed in the usual way by challenging the prosecution to put her to the question. Thus this case is not in point. The leading case upon which Guggenheim chiefly relies is the Herodes murder trial.[8] He has shown conclusively that there was no challenge in the case.[9] Naturally the defendant was suspected of murder when Herodes disappeared so mysteriously, but not until after the torture of the foreigner.[10] This foreigner, and a slave returning to Mytilene in a blood-stained boat in which Herodes and the defendant had been drinking at Methymna, were arrested, in all probability as suspects. The slave was a member of the crew of the

[1] D. 48:18; Lys. 1:16.
[2] Lys. 1:18.
[3] P. 29.
[4] P. 31.
[5] Pp. 890, 893.
[6] D. 48:15.
[7] Lys. 1:18.
[8] Ant. 5.
[9] Guggenheim, p. 30.
[10] Ant. 5:55; cf. 25; Guggenheim, p. 31.

vessel, but did not belong either to Herodes or to the defendant.[1] The torture of the freeman revealed nothing. After purchasing the slave, they tortured him. At first he implicated the defendant; he confessed that he had assisted him in slaying Herodes and in disposing of the body; but afterwards he denied all knowledge of the affair.[2] Finding that the slave could not be relied upon, they rejected the challenge to torture him,[3] and finally put him to death without due process of law.

It is well to remember, in this connection, that the slave, according to one of his confessions, was implicated in the murder, and that he was in the power of Athenians, living in Mytilene shortly after the unsuccessful revolt. There is every indication that the slave was properly an informer, as indeed he is frequently called throughout the speech.[4] Two courses were open to the prosecution, on finding that the confession of the slave attached grave suspicion to the defendant: they might have accepted the challenge to hand him over to the defendant, and had his answers produced before the jury; or they might have used him as an informer, and introduced him as such into the court.[5] The jury might use any means they wished to assure themselves of the truth of his story.[6] But, having put the slave to death, they were unable to proceed to the end with his information by producing him in court; and there is nowhere in the speech any indication that the slave's confession was before the jury in any form apart from its recital in the accuser's speech, while it is twice mentioned as the ground upon which the prosecutors base their confidence in the defendant's guilt.[7]

But even if the slave's answers were produced in court, Guggenheim's conclusion[8] could scarcely be regarded as a correct statement of the regular Athenian practice. He does not take into account the unusual circumstances of the case. The public sentiment of Athens was at that time somewhat inflamed against the Mytileneans. It would therefore be unwise to infer that a method of procedure which Athenian citizens felt they could employ against a Mytilenean defendant in a hard case was the regular practice. Nor does he attach sufficient importance to the vigorous objections of the defendant.

[1] Ant. 5:47. [2] Ant. 5:33, 39. [3] Ant. 5:34.

[4] Ant. 5:34, 38. The defendant's assumption that the slave would have been produced in court shows that he regarded him as an informer, for in no other capacity could a slave appear in court. (Ant. 5:46.)

[5] Ant. 5:46; cf. Guggenheim, p. 7.

[6] And. 1:11, for a means of testing a slave's information.

[7] Ant. 5:34, 52; cf. 39. [8] Guggenheim, p. 31.

Not only did a master seek to avail himself of the information which his slaves might acquire in the regular course of their service, but he even purposely put them in positions where they could gain information that would be useful in a particular suit.[1]

A challenge to examine a slave by torture indicated the conditions of the examination. It might be proposed to take evidence on a particular point to be submitted to the jury, or to settle the whole case according to the answers of the slave.[2]

This view has been disputed by Headlam,[3] who says: "There are no cases which clearly state that the answers of slaves under torture obtained by a *πρόκλησις* could be brought before a jury." This position he modified somewhat in his second article, in answer to the criticisms of Thompson,[4] by admitting that some of the passages brought forward by Thompson were vague and might support either side of the argument.[5] Without discussing Headlam's interpretation of these passages in detail, I shall only remark that they are by no means convincing, and proceed to cite two cases not before noticed in this discussion. The first and most conclusive proof that slave evidence could come before a jury is found in Isocrates: *ὁρῶ δὲ καὶ ὑμᾶς . . . . οὐδὲν πιστότερον οὐδ' ἀληθέστερον βασάνου νομίζοντας, καὶ μάρτυρας μὲν ἡγουμένους οἷόν τ' εἶναι καὶ τῶν μὴ γεγενημένων παρασκευάσασθαι, τὰς δὲ βασάνους φανερῶς ἐπιδεικνύναι, ὁπότεροι τἀληθῆ λέγουσιν. ἃ οὗτος εἰδὼς ἠβουλήθη εἰκάζειν ὑμᾶς περὶ τοῦ πράγματος μᾶλλον ἢ σαφῶς εἰδέναι.*[6] This passage should leave no doubt as to the practice in the matter of slave evidence. To the same effect is a passage in Demosthenes,[7] which should be read in conjunction with the passages from Isæus and Lycurgus. Sometimes the questions to be asked were specified in a general way, and a person called *βασανιστής* superintended the torture and assessed the damages inflicted on the slave as agreed upon. The *βασανιστής* might be one of the parties.[8]

If a challenge was delivered at the *ἀνάκρισις*, an adjournment to take the answers was allowed. But if the challenge contemplated the settlement of the case without further recourse to law, it could be delivered at any time

[1] D. 29:11, 21.

[2] A number of illustrative passages are collected in M. S. L., p. 893.

[3] *Classical Review*, Vol. VII, p. 1; Vol. VIII, p. 136.

[4] *Ibid.*, Vol. VIII, p. 136.

[5] Lys. 7:37; D. 30:35; Isæ. 8:10; Lyc. 1:28.

[6] Isoc. 17:54.

[7] D. 53:24.

[8] Ant. 1:10; cf. M. S. L., p. 895, regarding the administration of torture by a private individual.

even in the court itself.[1] Unreasonable delay in making a challenge was open to the suspicion of its being intended merely to delay proceedings.[2] Æschines[3] even proposed by challenge to have a slave tortured in the court. Relying on this passage and on another in Demosthenes,[4] some have concluded that it was possible to torture a slave in court.[5] But Apollodorus in his suit against Stephanus distinctly says: *βασανίζειν οὐκ ἔστιν ἐναντίον ὑμῶν.* Considerable ingenuity is displayed by Guggenheim in reconciling these passages. His conclusion is: "Wir nehmen gerne an, dass dem Redner es genügte, dass Folterung vor Gericht nicht gewöhnlich war, um für seinen Zweck behaupten zu können, sie kommen vor Gericht gar nicht vor."[6] But as Sandys has pointed out,[7] Æschines simply proposed, by means of a challenge, which was rejected by Demosthenes, to torture the slave. And, furthermore, the consent of the court was required, as the proviso *ἂν κελεύητε* shows. The real solution of the difficulty is simply that, with the consent of an opponent and the concurrence of the court, anything could be done, be it never so irregular according to the regular practice. The answers of the slaves might be taken down and sealed, or they could be proved by the depositions of any persons who were present.[8]

A slave's evidence is often praised, and occasionally depreciated,[9] but rarely, if ever, actually introduced as the result of a challenge.[10] There was an undoubted shrinking from handing over a slave to be tortured, for fear he would make his answers suit the desires of the person who had control of the torture.[11] On the other hand, men confessed to be unwilling

1 D. 47:13, 16; Guggenheim, pp. 34 ff.

2 D. 54:26 ff.

3 Æsch. 2:126.

4 In reference to the passage from Demosthenes *καίτοι ἔδει αὐτόν, ... κληρουμένων τῶν δικαστηρίων κομίσαντα τὴν ἄνθρωπον, ... κελεύειν ἐμέ, εἰ βουλοίμην, βασανίζειν, καὶ μάρτυρας τοὺς δικαστὰς εἰσιόντας ποιεῖσθαι ὡς ἕτοιμός ἐστι παραδοῦναι* (D. 47:17), Sandys says: "But it would be idle to suppose that the passage proves that the torture might take place in open court; all that is meant is that the defendant might have produced the girl when the court was about to sit, challenged the plaintiff to 'question' her, and called the jurors to bear witness that he was ready to hand her over to be tortured in the usual manner and not in the public court."

5 M. S. L., p. 894; Pauly–Wissowa, *s. v. βάσανος*; Smith, *Dict. Ant.*, *s. v. Tormentum*; Guggenheim, pp. 36 ff.

6 P. 37.

7 Note on D. 45:16.

8 D. 53:24, 25.

9 Cf. Ant. 5:31 ff. with Ant. 6:25. For a full collection of *loci insignes* on the subject of torture see Dobree, *Advers.*, p. 317; cf. Arist., *Rhet.*, I, 15, 26.

10 For the slave evidence in Ant. 5 see p. 70; there was no challenge in this case.

11 Ant. 5:32.

to accept a slave for examination, fearing the natural bias in favor of his master.[1]

There are three instances of the acceptance of a challenge, but in each case some disagreement arose which prevented the contract from being carried out.[2]

A rather curious effect of slave evidence, according to Isæus and Demosthenes, was that it would protect a witness who gave similar testimony from a prosecution for perjury.[3]

Citizens were not liable to be tortured;[4] but we have instances of persons who were foreigners, or had lost their civic rights, being tortured in the case of serious crimes.[5] A master who had freed a slave apparently retained the right to hand him over to be questioned, but Demosthenes says that it would be impious to do so.[6]

CHAPTER XIII

OATHS

The evidentiary oath is characteristic of society in its primitive form, when mankind had strong faith in the avenging powers of an offended deity. The Anglo-Saxons sometimes allowed an accused man to clear himself by an oath;[7] and in Massachusetts Colony a white man's oath was deemed sufficient answer to the accusation of an Indian.[8] In Greece the introduction of the evidentiary oath was popularly referred to Rhadamanthus, who required the two parties at issue to take an oath respecting the points in dispute. As no one in those days would dare to take a false oath, only one party took the oath, and the case was speedily settled.[9] An

[1] Lys. 4:16. Professor Mahaffy (*Social Life in Greece*, p. 241) thinks that the slave was liable to be put to death by his master, if he gave evidence unfavorable to him. He bases his views on Ant. 6:25. Isoc. 17:55, which he does not cite, seems to confirm his view.

[2] D. 47:6 ff.; 37:42; Isoc. 17:15.

[3] D. 29:21: *ἤθελον παραδοῦναι τὸν παῖδα . . . . οὐχὶ μαρτύρων ἀπορῶν . . . . ἀλλ' ἵνα μὴ τούτους αἰτιῷτο τὰ ψευδῆ μαρτυρεῖν, ἀλλὰ τὸ πιστὸν ἐκ τῆς βασάνου τούτοις ὑπάρχοι*; cf. D. 47:5; Isæ. 8:10; Lyc. 1:28.

[4] And. 1:43.

[5] See passages cited by Thalheim in Pauly-Wissowa, *Real.-Encyc.*, *s. v.* *βάσανος*.

[6] D. 29:39.

[7] Thayer, *Evidence*, pp. 24, 25.

[8] I. *Prov. Laws Mass.*, 151 (1693–94). 3. Æsch., *Eumen.*, 432.

[9] Plato, *Laws*, 948 B; cf. Gilbert, pp. 464 ff.

oath of this kind appears in Homer;[1] and in Æschylus, Orestes was challenged to an evidentiary oath, but refused it, as he would thus have been prevented from pleading justification for the deed.[2] Solon restricted the evidentiary oath to cases where no other evidence was available. In case both parties took an oath, the jurors had to decide who swore the truth. By the time of the Orators the evidentiary character of the party oath had disappeared, and both parties, as a matter of course, swore to their pleadings. Different theories have been advanced to account for this practice.[3] The only way in which an evidentiary oath could be brought before the court was by means of challenges; and, as these were very rarely accepted, the evidentiary oath ceased to be of much importance, except in respect of arguments drawn from an opponent's refusal to accept the challenge;[4] for the Greeks shrank from taking an evidentiary oath except in important matters. We know of only one instance of the acceptance of a challenge to settle a point at issue by an evidentiary oath; and in that case the oath was taken before an arbitrator.[5]

It is commonly believed that the regular rule for determining the competency of witnesses holds in respect of an evidentiary oath, except in the case of parties to the suit and women.[6] No account seems to be taken of the fact that there are two distinct classes of evidentiary oaths. By far the more numerous class comprises those oaths that were intended to settle the question at issue without recourse to a court of law. Waiving the question as to whether such oaths can properly be classed as evidentiary matter, we may at once conclude that in extrajudicial proceedings any person would be competent to take these oaths. But other considerations present themselves when an evidentiary oath before the jury is contemplated. Here we must assume that the ordinary rules regarding the competency of regular witnesses apply, unless it can be distinctly shown that exceptions were allowed. But, so far as women are concerned, there is no indication in the authorities that they could take an evidentiary oath in court. Of the references to such an oath, one recites that it was taken before an arbitrator, while another mentions a challenge to take it at an arbitration.[7] In two cases there is no express reference to an arbitration,

1 Iliad, 23, 573 ff.

2 Eumenides, 432 ff. Cf. Bréhier, pp. 91 ff.

3 Gilbert, p. 466; M. S. L., pp. 826, 898 ff.; Rhode, *Psyche*, 244, n. 2; Philippi, pp. 88 ff.

4 D. 33:14; 41:41; 49:65.

5 D. 40:10.

6 M. S. L., p. 899. Mederle, pp. 26, 28, agrees with M. S. L., while Platner, Vol. II, p. XXXVIII, is very doubtful in regard to women.

7 D. 40:10; Isæ. 12:9.

nor is an oath in court in any way implied. But both these cases were subject to arbitration, so that they afford no support for the view that the oath could be administered to a woman in court.[1] As a matter of fact the taking of an evidentiary oath would settle the questions involved, and they would not come before the court at all. The result is that where an oath in court was in contemplation there is not sufficient evidence to warrant the view that the rule of competency was ever relaxed except in the case of parties to a suit.[2] Demosthenes' statement that challenges were devised for those transactions which could not be brought before the jury points to the same conclusion. Just as a slave could not be tortured in court so a woman could not be sworn in court.[3]

A litigant might tender his own evidentiary oath or offer to accept that of his opponent; or the oath of a third party might be offered. Demosthenes, the speaker in Aphobus v. Phanus, offers to take an oath in the interest of his client, Phanus, who had been Demosthenes' witness in Demosthenes v. Aphobus, and was now being prosecuted by Aphobus for perjury.[4] In the same speech he challenges the plaintiff to accept his mother's oath in regard to the manumission of Milyas.[5] The witnesses, too, offered to take an oath on the heads of their children.[6] These challenges always contemplated a peculiarly solemn and impressive oath.[7] The oath, together with the challenge, was usually included in the documents of the case and produced in court;[8] but a challenge that had not been accepted might be brought to the attention of the jury in the speech without the production of documentary evidence.[9] The oath could be administered in court, except in the case of women, and the challenger had the right to determine its form.[10]

All witnesses in cases before the Areopagus were sworn at the preliminary investigation. This oath, like that in cases of disclaimer, was in character similar to the evidentiary oath.[11] In respect of the regular oath administered to witnesses in other cases, our authorities are almost silent. Demosthenes twice mentions its administration by one of the parties to his opponent's witnesses at an arbitration.[12] Whether witnesses were regularly sworn is a matter of dispute. Lipsius properly takes the view that the oath

[1] D. 29:26, 33; 55:27; cf. Platner, Vol. II, p. xxxviii. For the woman's oath mentioned in D. 47:70 ff., see above, p. 33, note 4.

[2] Cf. Mederle, p. 26.

[3] D 46:12.

[4] D. 29:52.

[5] D. 29:33; cf. Isæ. 12:9.

[6] D. 29:54.

[7] M. S. L., p. 900, n. 383.

[8] M. S. L., p. 900.

[9] D. 29:54.

[10] Mederle, p. 26.

[11] Ant. 5:12; Lys. 4:4; cf. Philippi, p. 87.

[12] D. 54:26; 45:57.

was not always exacted, though one of his arguments is by no means convincing. In two cases an oath to be sworn in court is mentioned. He concludes that in such cases there could have been no ordinary witness oath, as that would involve two oaths from the witness regarding the same matter. But as the proposed second oath was more impressive in character, and was administered only with the consent of the witness, there does not seem to be any good reason why he might not take both oaths.[1]

The almost complete silence of the Orators regarding the oath is a clear indication that it was of slight importance. Once it is mentioned by Apollodorus as a mere incident. Stephanus, it was alleged, took the opportunity to steal an affidavit while Apollodorus was engaged in swearing a witness.[2] In the other case, Conon, the defendant, was charged by the plaintiff with swearing the witnesses one by one for the purpose of obstructing and prolonging the proceedings before the arbitrator.[3] The tone of the passage suggests that Conon was at least exacting to the uttermost his rights in the matter.

It is to be observed that the oath was not administered by the magistrate, but by one of the parties. Since the administration of the oath to an opponent's witnesses was of the nature of a privilege, it could be omitted at will by either party. So far as we can see, there was no particular object to be gained by it. A suit for perjury was the result, not of a false oath but of false evidence. Plato's abolition of all oaths for witnesses except in case of a disclaimer, and the entire absence of witness oaths from some Greek legal systems, show that the oath was not felt to be essential. The disuse of the evidentiary oath, and the purely formal character of the preliminary oath of the parties confirming the pleadings, point to the same conclusion.[4]

In a number of cases in the Orators it is difficult to see how a witness could have been sworn in the regular way. When the plaintiff in Euxitheus v. Eubulides challenged anyone to come forward and give testimony if he is not speaking the truth, he makes no mention of administering an oath.[5] Nor is there any mention of a witness oath where reluctant witnesses had the alternative presented to them of giving evidence or of taking the oath of disclaimer.[6] The defendant in the Herodes murder trial asserts distinctly that the witnesses for the prosecution were unsworn.[7] This has been very plausibly explained as a forceful statement of the fact that the

[1] M. S. L., p. 885. [2] D. 45:57. [3] D. 54:26.

[4] Plato, *Laws*, 936 *e;* Gilbert, p. 467, n. 2. [5] D. 57:61.

[6] Isæ. 2:33; Æsch., 1:47; cf. *supra*, p. 43.

[7] Ant. 5:12.

witness had not taken the usual solemn oath required in murder trials;[1] but it is not improbable that the statement of Antiphon is literally true. In this, and in all other cases in which there was no arbitration, there was no opportunity to administer an oath to an opponent's witnesses, since they were not obliged to present themselves at the preliminary investigation.[2]

Several instances of oaths sworn in court in the presence of the jury occur which cannot be satisfactorily explained by assuming that they are in compliance with a challenge.[3] A considerable number of witnesses in Euxitheus v. Eubulides took an oath in court to confirm their testimony. There is no indication that the oath was in accordance with a challenge from the other side. The case was an appeal from the decision of a deme disfranchising the plaintiff. As the witnesses were relatives of the plaintiff and deeply interested in his fate, one is led to surmise that the oaths were purely gratuitous on the part of the witnesses.[4] It is difficult to believe that, if there had been a challenge, no trace of it would be found in the speech. How could the speaker suppress a note of triumph over the acceptance of a challenge by his witness?[5] Several of Æschines' witnesses appear to have voluntarily taken an oath in court in the same way.[6]

But another phase of this question is presented by the proposed oath of a witness in Apollodorus v. Timotheus. It appears that the plaintiff, suspecting that one of his witnesses was adverse, demanded that he give his testimony under solemn oath. The witness had failed to appear at the arbitration, and Apollodorus had instituted a suit for damages against him. When the original case came to trial, Apollodorus suggested that he come forward and say under oath whether he borrowed a certain sum of money for Timotheus.[7] His failure to appear, after repeated promises, would naturally give rise to a suspicion that he had been tampered with and might prove adverse. It is, however, possible that the proposed oath is an evidentiary oath.

In brief a witness might take a solemn oath in court (1) as the result of a challenge; (2) of his own accord, to make his evidence more impressive in the interest of a friend; (3) possibly at the instance of the party

[1] M. S. L., p. 885.

[2] *Supra*, p. 49.

[3] Mederle, p. 33.

[4] D. 57:22, 44.

[5] Mederle (p. 33) denies the possibility of such an oath's being taken legally without the concurrence of the other side; but there is no sufficient reason to be found why a witness could not of his own accord call down destruction on himself in case the affidavit he had subscribed to is not true.

[6] Æsch. 2:156.

[7] D. 49:20; cf. *ante*, p. 43.

for whom he appeared, as the result of a suspicion that he would prove adverse.

Either of the parties might swear to the truth of his statements in court without a challenge. The defendant in Ariston v. Conon is said by Ariston to be prepared to take an exceedingly sensational oath on the heads of his children. To counteract the effect of this expected oath, he reads a challenge that he was willing to stake the matter on a lawful oath, and then swears by all the deities, with imprecations on his own head, that his statements regarding the injuries he suffered are true.[1] In Sophocles' *Antigone*, a messenger offered to undergo the ordeal by fire and to take an oath that his tale was true; but neither this passage nor the one in Demosthenes' Ariston v. Conon, usually cited in connection with the passage from *Antigone*, affords any indication that the ordeal by fire was in use in historical times either for parties or for witnesses.[2]

CHAPTER XIV

EXPERT EVIDENCE

Caillemer, after enumerating Aristotle's familiar divisions of πίστεις ἄτεχνοι, remarks: "Il est permis d'en douter et de croire que la procédure athénienne admettait d'autres preuves directs, telle que l'expertise."[3] On the other hand, the statement of Lipsius[4] "dass sie [die Aussagen von Sachverständigen] auf die Weise, wie bei uns, im attischen Process gar nicht vorgekommen seien, und dass Sachverständige, wenn man sie gebrauchte, nur als Zeugen betrachtet wurden," is probably too conservative. There are two instances, at least, in which the expert knowledge of the physician was required. It is doubtless true, as Lipsius observes, that the Orators were unconscious of the difference between an expert

[1] D. 54:38–41; cf. 55:24; 32:31; cf. Mederle, p. 27, for the oath of Conon.

[2] Sophocles, *Antig.*, 264, 265, with Jebb's note; D. 54:40, with Sandys' note; cf. Dareste, *Demosthenes*, Vol. II, p. 243. For a discussion of ordeals among the Greeks see Bréhier, pp. 94 ff.

[3] Daremberg et Saglio, *Dict. des antiq.*, *s. v.* ἀνάκρισις. In one of the passages dealing with a prosecution for wounding with intent, which he cites as an example of expert testimony, the physician, who told of his being asked by the plaintiff to make a superficial scalp wound, is in no sense an expert witness. His evidence is a statement of fact and not an opinion. (D. 40:33).

[4] M. S. L., p. 866.

and a regular witness, but this does not alter the essential character of such a witness.

The defendant in the third Tetralogy of Antiphon declares that the deceased died, not as a result of the wound, but by reason of improper treatment at the hands of the attending physician. Witnesses are introduced to substantiate the statement.[1] Had this been a real case, we should no doubt have seen the evidence of two groups of physicians pitted against each other. A physician is called in Ariston v. Conon to prove that, but for the discharge of blood which was collected as the result of an internal hemorrhage, his patient would have died.[2] This is an undoubted instance of expert evidence which no one but a professional man could have given. Its value depended entirely upon the professional skill and experience of the witness. We have here the real beginnings of expert evidence, though the meager deposition of the Athenian witness bears little resemblance to the evidence extracted from an expert witness in a modern court.

There is a number of cases in which expert testimony might have been used to advantage. In view of the number of frauds in connection with wills and other documents, it is remarkable that some attempts were not made to expose them by an appeal to the handwriting.[3] There are references to two different slaves, who, it was said, would readily detect any changes made in the documents they had written.[4]

There are two cases in Lysias in which expert testimony might have proved useful. The cripple who appealed to the jury to trust their own eyes as to his physical condition probably found it unnecessary to produce the evidence of a physician;[5] but it would have been to the advantage of his accusers if they could have produced a physician to prove that his apparent weakness did not incapacitate him. And an expert valuator would have been of great service in determining the value of goods in dispute.[6] External evidence, no doubt, led to the conclusion that the blood found in the boat in which it was supposed Herodes met a violent death was not human blood.[7]

[1] Ant., *Tetral.* Γ, δ, 8.

[2] D. 54:12; cf. 47:67, where laymen as well as a physician are called to testify to the condition of a person who had been wounded.

[3] Isæ. 4:13; Ant. 5:53; Isoc. 17:23 ff.

[4] D. 29:21; 33:17 ff.

[5] Lys. 24:14.

[6] Lys. 17:7.

[7] Ant. 5:29. There was, of course, no possibility of determining the nature of the stains by an examination.

CHAPTER XV

REAL EVIDENCE

Real evidence has been defined as "all evidence that is addressed directly to the senses of the jury without the intervention of the testimony of witnesses, as where various things are exhibited in court."[1] Persons also are included in respect of such qualities as belong to them in common with things.

It is interesting to note that Isocrates virtually defines real evidence as that which appeals to the eyes. In speaking of the woman who was produced in court to refute fourteen witnesses who had testified that she was dead, he remarks: *τοὺς μὲν γὰρ ἄλλους ἐκ τῶν λεγομένων κρίνετε, τὴν δὲ τούτου μαρτυρίαν, ὅτι ψευδὴς ἦν, εἶδον οἱ δικάζοντες.*[2] He is fully alive to the effectiveness of this bit of real evidence; but the Orators in general paid little or no attention to the production of real evidence.

Several other examples of the use of persons as real evidence occur. In Apollodorus v. Nicostratus there is a proposal that the defendant exhibit to the jury the scars which were left by the leg-irons which he as a prisoner had worn. It is not likely that the defendant furnished this corroboration for the statements of his opponent.[3] Demosthenes twice produced men in court who were incompetent witnesses. One was a slave who was produced to show that he was incapable of committing the assault in question.[4] The other was a man who had been disfranchised by the wrongful act of the defendant in the case. He was produced to show the jury the enormity of the crime—a freeman deprived of the right to complain of his wrongs.[5]

Almost no use is made of things for evidentiary purposes. Instruments with which persons were wounded or slain were never produced in court. In fact, they are rarely mentioned. The slayer of Eratosthenes, in his account passes lightly over the actual killing, without mentioning the weapon he used;[6] the prosecution in the Herodes case suggested that a stone was the weapon used;[7] and in a case of assault a piece of an earthen vessel is mentioned as the weapon with which the wound was inflicted.[8]

1 *American and English Encyclopædia of Law*, Vol. XI, p. 536.

2 Isoc. 18:56 ff.

3 D. 53:8; cf. Lys. 24:14.

4 D. 37:44.

5 D. 21:95; cf. D. 39:27; Æsch. 1:49, where the speakers remark on the apparent age of persons who are before the jury. Cf. Herodas, *Mimes*, 2:65, where Myrtale is introduced to show the jury how she had been maltreated by the defendant.

6 Lys. 1:26.

7 Ant. 5:26.

8 Lys. 4:7.

Mantitheus v. Bœotus[1] affords an interesting instance of a document used as real evidence. Mantitheus tried to have his half-brother, Bœotus, compelled to relinquish the name "Mantitheus" which he claimed, and in order to show that his name really was Bœotus, according to his own admission, he produced the pleadings to show that he had accepted service in the suit and appealed against an arbitrator's decision under that name. These documents are not introduced as evidence of statements or recitals contained in them, but simply to show that the name "Bœotus" occurs. So a will produced in court that the jury might inspect the seals in order to assure themselves of its authenticity is real evidence.[2]

English practice allows a witness to refer to letters or memoranda to refresh his memory. Naturally there is no Athenian parallel to this in the case of a witness, though Demosthenes on one occasion read from a memorandum or diary.[3] The speaker in Eubulides v. Macartatus proposed to aid the jury in comprehending the genealogy of the claimants for an estate by reducing it to writing; but it did not seem feasible, because those who sat toward the rear would be unable to see it; and consequently he gave up the idea.[4] The only modern analogy to such a proceeding is the production of a plan or map of the locality where the events in question took place. Such a plan or map is produced by a witness who has made it, and the necessary explanations are given. We do find the defendant in a suit involving damages caused by a ditch regretting that the jury was not familiar with the locality, but there is no suggestion of making a map of the locality, or of having the jury view it, as may be done now [5]

CHAPTER XVI

ADVOCATES' SPEECHES

It was the regular custom for litigants to have advocates (*συνήγοροι*) speak in their behalf, and it was considered a matter of great importance to have the support of clever speakers or of men of influence.[6] Apparently no one could appear as an advocate without the permission of the court.[7] Although the law forbade them to take pay, Demosthenes maintains that the rich man had the advantage over his poorer opponent in securing assistance of this kind.[8]

[1] D. 39:37. [2] D. 45:17. [3] D. 21:130. [4] D. 43:18. [5] D. 55:9.

[6] D. 21:112; 58:59; cf. M. S. L., pp. 920–25, for a complete list of authorities; Hyper. 6:11 ff. is especially good.

[7] D. 34:52; 59:14. [8] D. 46:26; 21:112.

In view of the suspicion attaching to the motives which led a man to appear as an advocate, it was important that he should explain why he championed the cause of a litigant. Relationship[1] or friendship for a man,[2] and hostility toward his opponent, are the usual motives.[3] Andocides was supported by advocates selected by members of his tribe.[4] Evidently a foreigner might be an advocate.[5]

The letter of Satyrus to the city of Athens, in reference to the affairs of a certain Sinopean whose father was in his service, properly belongs here. It was read to the jury by the Sinopean in his suit against Pasion, the banker.[6] This is the only Athenian example of a practice which was so much abused at Rome that it was forbidden by Pompey's laws in 52 B. C.[7]

The introduction of female relatives and children into court to arouse compassion is but another phase of advocacy.[8]

Advocates' speeches ranged all the way from a well-ordered treatment of the facts already brought out, to mere rhetorical and emotional appeals.[9] Sometimes the speech took the form of a request for a verdict favorable to the client as a recognition of the public services of the speaker.[10]

It was inevitable that in many cases an advocate's appeal should more or less closely resemble original oral testimony. When a friend undertakes the entire case for a man who does not feel complete confidence in his ability to conduct his own case, his statements, as a matter of fact, differ from a regular deposition only in the form in which they are presented. Unlike regular speeches, they are uncorroborated by the evidence of witnesses. The same man might be both advocate and witness.[11] The speech of Isæus as the advocate of Hagnon and Hagnotheus, claimants for the estate of Nicostratus, is a careful *résumé* of the whole case as developed by the regular speech and the evidence.[12] It bears a striking resemblance to the address of a modern lawyer to the jury, until the latter part, where his statements about the characters of the parties to the suit closely approximate a deposition.[13] So the advocate of Callias testifies in effect

1 D. 32:31.

2 Isoc. 21:1.

3 D. 58:4.

4 And. 1:150.

5 D. 49:22.

6 Isoc. 17:52.

7 Greenidge, *Legal Procedure of Cicero's Time*, pp. 490, 491, 592.

8 D. 48:57. Cf. Hyper., *Frag.*, 60.

9 Isæ. 4; Lys. 27:12.

10 Lys. 12:86.

11 Æsch. 2:170, 184.

12 Isæ. 4:18, 20, 26.

13 Isæ. 4:27 ff. His appeal to the jury for corroboration does not alter his character as a virtual witness.

to the public services of his client.[1] The unattested speech in Isocrates is largely made up of hearsay; but some of the statements are made on the speaker's own knowledge, without any attempt at corroboration. No one was so well aware as he of the deposit of the furniture of his client with himself. And he may very well have known of the mortgage on the house and the sending of the slaves beyond Attica.[2]

That these speeches were common in all kinds of cases is obvious from the number of appeals for assistance that are preserved.[3] It is safe to assume that in most cases the speakers bore testimony to the good character of their clients, and thus resembled to some extent those modern witnesses who are called solely to establish the fact that the accused bore a good reputation in his neighborhood.

The frequent attempts to discourage and discredit in advance those who were likely to be advocates show that their speeches were not without considerable effect. Demosthenes in his speech against Meidias makes the point that, as Eubulus, a prospective advocate, did not assist Meidias at the trial before the assembly, he cannot be convinced of the justice of his cause.[4]

CHAPTER XVII

THE PERSONAL KNOWLEDGE OF THE JURORS

It was inevitable that in a numerous Athenian jury there should be many who were more or less familiar with the facts in the cases they adjudicated. Nor was this felt by litigants to be a disadvantage. Indeed, Demosthenes regrets that his differences with his guardians had to be settled by men who were unfamiliar with the facts, rather than by the arbitration of mutual friends. It might even happen that a man went into the jury with his mind fully made up before he heard any of the evidence.[5] Plato would require a juryman who had special knowledge of the facts of a case to leave the jury and become a witness.[6] There are in the Orators numerous appeals to the knowledge of the jurors on various matters.[7] They are virtually witnesses, and are often spoken of as such.[8] A speaker could have no better corroborative witnesses than the men who

[1] Lys. 5.

[2] Isoc. 21:2–3.

[3] Cf. D. 58:70; Isoc. 20:22.

[4] D. 21:206 ff.; cf. 58:53; 48:36.

[5] Lys. 6:54; D. 27:1.

[6] Plato, *Laws*, 937 A.

[7] D. 34:50; 44:66; Ant. 6:25.

[8] D. 21:80; Lys. 10:1.

sat on the jury.[1] A client of Lysias relied entirely on the jury for confirmation of what he said,[2] and produced no witnesses. Sometimes it is said that the entire jury knows that the speaker's words are true. But even under these circumstances, witnesses are often introduced, though at the risk of trying the patience of the court.[3] If only part of the jurors know, it was customary to ask them to inform those who sat near them.[4] It was chiefly in respect of matters that were of public interest that the jury was called upon for corroboration. A curious instance of negative evidence occurs in this connection, when it is taken for granted that, if no one in such a numerous body has ever heard of a thing, it cannot be true.[5]

A litigant might even take the precaution to bring a matter to the notice of men who would be jurymen, with a view to appealing to their knowledge afterward. This could easily be done in the case of a challenge delivered to an opponent in the presence of those who were being impaneled as jurors.[6] The plaintiff in Ariston v. Conon suggests that Conon should have gone to see in what condition he was after the assault, accompanied by some members of the Areopagus as witnesses in case death resulted.[7] It was immaterial that the knowledge of some of the jurors was from hearsay.[8] It was a favorite trick, according to Demosthenes,[9] of those who could produce no witnesses to refer to the matter as being familiar to the jurors, when in fact they knew nothing about it. Each juror, supposing that his neighbor knew, would be more or less impressed by the statement.

The modern English practice of selecting a jury of men who are unacquainted with the issue to be tried, or at least entirely free from prejudice, is a comparatively late development. Well on in the eighteenth century we find juries deciding cases on their own knowledge.[10] In the early history of the English jury its efficiency depended on its knowledge; for the jurors were summoned by the judge for the purpose of answering certain questions which he put to them.[11] Knowledge of the matter in dispute was thus a prime requisite.

[1] D. 21:18.

[2] Lys. 24:5.

[3] Lys. 12:61; D. 57:33.

[4] And. 1:37; D. 47:44; 50:3.

[5] D. 35:35; 37:56.

[6] D. 47:16, 17.

[7] D. 54:28.

[8] Ant. 5:71.

[9] D. 40:53.

[10] Thayer, pp. 94, 170.

[11] Thayer, pp. 47 ff.

CHAPTER XVIII

IMPEACHMENT OF WITNESSES

Singularly few convincing objections to the credibility of witnesses are to be found in the speeches of the Orators. Many rhetorical attacks occur such as are recommended by Aristotle and the Rhetoricians. These are conveniently collected and characterized by Volkmann,[1] and need not be discussed here.

One of the most effective ways of assailing the credibility of a witness is to show that his accounts of the transaction in question have varied materially. Thus evidence is brought to show that the sole witness of the defendant in Chrysippus v. Phormio had formerly, in the presence of witnesses, denied the receipt of the money which he now alleges was intrusted to him for the plaintiff, but lost in the wreck of his vessel. When the case came up before the arbitrator, he revoked his earlier statement, explaining that he did not know what he was doing when he made it. The plaintiff accounts for this change of front on the part of the witness Lampis by saying that he received a share of the money which Phormio was seeking to withhold.[2] Antiphon comments on the unreliability of the statements of the slave who had told two different stories of a murder.[3]

There is no more effective way of discrediting a witness than by proving conclusively that his evidence is false. The best example of this occurs in Isocrates, where a woman was produced in court to confound fourteen witnesses who had testified that she was dead.[4]

Ariston v. Conon furnishes a good instance of discrediting the evidence of witnesses by proving, both by appeals to the knowledge of the jury and by depositions of witnesses, that they were guilty of other crimes and misdemeanors. The chief witnesses of the defendants were shown to be boon companions of his; and not a few of the jurymen are said to be familiar with their real character, which is inconsistent with their assumption of a Spartan austerity of manner during the day. Finally evidence is produced to prove that they were frequently guilty of house-breaking and assaults on the streets after nightfall. The inference that such men would not scruple to resort to falsehood differs fundamentally from an attempt to persuade a jury that evidence is suspicious because it is given by a man's friends who have not been shown to be guilty of wrongdoing in other

[1] Volkmann, p. 187.

[2] D. 34:11, 18 ff., 46.

[3] Ant. 5:33 ff.

[4] Isoc. 18:53 ff.

respects.[1] We hear in Lysias of a plaintiff who charged an opposing witness with being a parricide.[2]

The attempt of Apollodorus to prove that Stephanus, whom he is prosecuting for perjury in the suit of Apollodorus v. Phormio, had stolen a deposition at a session of the arbitrator's court, is strictly an attack on the credibility of Stephanus as a witness in the former suit, though it is calculated to prejudice him in his character as defendant in the present suit.[3]

The Athenians' suspicion of the testimony of a party to an action, which is shown by their not allowing a man to be a witness in his own behalf, is occasionally appealed to for the purpose of discrediting a witness who is alleged to have an interest in the subject-matter of the litigation.[4] An exceedingly effective way of discrediting a witness was to show that he had no opportunity of knowing what is contained in his deposition. Such evidence is really hearsay.[5]

Such weaknesses in evidence are most readily and easily exposed in a modern law court by means of cross-examination; and a passage in Isæus[6] shows how effectively this method would have exposed the pretensions of the witness, if he had been obliged to answer the question which Isæus suggests. In addition to the manifold resources of the cross-examination, the English lawyer can impeach a witness by proving that he is guilty of crimes or misdemeanors for which he has been punished, or that he is so untrustworthy that men are willing to swear that they would not believe him on oath.

The prominence of the evidentiary matter in a speech made it of considerable importance to impair the veracity of an opponent.[7] Not only must a man prove his own case, but he must expose the falsehoods of his opponent, which was a difficult task in the case of a man of good character who was also a clever speaker.[8]

No more damaging impeachment of an opponent's credit is to be found in the Orators than occurs in a case by Isocrates, where evidence is produced to show that the plaintiff, Callimachus, had in a former suit been convicted of perjury in open court.[9] Of a similar nature is the claim of the plaintiff in Apollodorus v. Timotheus that the jurors are well aware that Timotheus had in the most public manner broken very solemn oaths.

1 D. 54:31–37. 2 Lys., 10:1 ff. 3 D. 45:57 ff.

4 D. 40:58. Cf. *supra*, p. 29, n. 3. 5 Isæ. 6:53 ff.; D. 40:59; D. 44:54.

6 Isæ. 6:53: *νῦν δὲ πῶς ἂν περιφανέστερον ἐξελεγχθείη τὰ ψευδῆ μεμαρτυρηκὼς ἢ εἴ τις αὐτὸν ἔροιτο "Ἀνδρόκλεις, πῶς οἶσθα Φιλοκτήμων' ὅτι οὔτε διέθετο οὔτε υἱὸν Χαιρέστρατον ἐποιήσατο;"*

7 Cf. Isæ. 5:8. 8 D. 52:1. 9 Isoc. 18:52 ff.

The avowed object of Apollodorus is to explain to the jury why he felt justified in refusing to accept the defendant's challenge to an oath; but its effect must have been to impair the jury's confidence in the reliability of his opponent's statements.[1] In one of his suits with Aphobus, Demosthenes was defending one of his witnesses who was being prosecuted for perjury, and he had the good fortune to destroy utterly the credit of Aphobus, the prosecutor, by proving that on a previous occasion he had himself given exactly the same evidence as he was now seeking to impeach.[2]

A man's veracity may also be impeached by evidence that he has made conflicting statements, or that his acts belie his words. Demosthenes, in his suit against Aphobus, showed that not only had he made contradictory statements, but that a comparison of the assertions of the guardians concerning the provisions of his father's will revealed material contradictions.[3] A good example of acts that belie words occurs in Antiphon's defense of the man charged with the murder of the chorus boy.[4] The prosecutor, as was well known, had associated publicly with the defendant, though, if their charge was true, they would have shunned him as being defiled. There are many alleged instances of inconsistencies between words and deeds which are not supported by evidence.

In behalf of the wards in their suit against Diogeiton grave suspicion was thrown upon the entire guardianship account by the fact that in one particular, regarding a contribution to the public service, the papers of the man who was joined with Diogeiton in the service showed that the amount expended was much smaller than the sum set down in the account.[5] The value of an opponent's statement might also be considerably impaired by proof that he had had no opportunity of knowing at first hand what he affirms or denies.[6] Demosthenes, in criticizing an opponent, enters a forcible protest against the practice of making assertions on hearsay.[7]

CHAPTER XIX

PERJURY

To judge from the number of references in the Orators to perjury, one would conclude that it was a comparatively common offense. Two instances will suffice to show both the lengths to which witnesses went in falsification and the shameless effrontery of those who profited by the

[1] D. 49:66; cf. 42:29. [2] D. 29:20 ff. [3] D. 27:42 ff.

[4] Ant. 6:39, 40, 45 ff.; cf. D. 31:4. [5] Lys. 32:26. [6] Ant. 1:28. [7] D. 57:4.

crime. Isocrates[1] tells of a case in which the perjury of fourteen witnesses, who had testified that a certain woman was dead, was completely exposed by the subsequent introduction into court of the woman herself; and the plaintiff in Callistratus v. Olympiodorus tells the jury, without a blush, how Olympiodorus, in a former suit in which both were interested, had, with his connivance, produced perjured evidence.[2]

Prosecutions for perjury were encouraged as well by the policy of the law, which imposed only a slight penalty on the prosecutor in case of failure,[3] as by the fact that in certain classes of cases a successful prosecution of a false witness was a step toward the setting aside of the judgment in the original case. The party who intended to prosecute his opponent's witness was required to give formal notice of his intention before a verdict was rendered.[4] From this requirement it would appear that the right to prosecute a false witness was not confined to the losing party. That such was in fact the case has been satisfactorily established.

Nor was the right to prosecute confined to the parties themselves; for in criminal cases it must often have occurred that the prosecution could not be conducted by the party who had suffered from the perjury. Doubtless, under those circumstances, a relative or any other citizen could prosecute the case;[5] and there are some indications, hitherto unnoticed, that even in civil cases third persons might freely denounce and prosecute witnesses. In Callistratus v. Olympiodorus it is recited that the plaintiff and the defendant in the present case, who were brothers-in-law, had both been claimants to the estate of one Conon; but they had reached an agreement[6] according to which Olympiodorus alone was to claim the whole estate and share it with Callistratus equally. The present suit was brought by Callistratus to compel his brother-in-law to pay over some moneys which he had secured from a slave of Conon subsequently to the division of the property. In an earlier suit against other claimants for the estate Olympiodorus had brought in witnesses who testified that Callistratus was paying rent to him for the house which had been assigned to him under the agreement as part of his share of the estate. Callistratus now proves, as an evidence of his good faith and his intention to abide by the contract which Olympiodorus had broken by refusing to divide all the property, that he allowed this evidence to go unchallenged.

The kind of interference in the suit here contemplated is clearly indicated by a technical word which otherwise is limited in the Orators to the formal

1 Isoc. 18:52 ff.; cf. 17:54. 2 D. 48:44. 3 D. 47:2.

4 Arist., *Const. of Athens*, col. 35, ll. 10 ff.

5 Rentzsch, pp. 30 ff. 6 D. 48:9, 29, 44.

denunciation of perjury,[1] and it is reasonable to suppose that Callistratus has in mind the first step in a prosecution for perjury. If he had the right to take the first step, he surely was competent to proceed with the charge and bring the witnesses to trial. Now, Callistratus was not really a party to the suit. In the eyes of the jury, which knew nothing of the compact between him and his brother-in-law, he was simply a relative of Conon's, and might have been one of the claimants for the property, if he had chosen; but as he had failed to do so openly, he was an entire stranger to the case; and yet he assumes that he might have prosecuted the witness for perjury. It is scarcely worth inquiring whether the right to prosecute was based upon an interest in the evidence in the way of possible damage which might result from it in case it was not challenged and proved to be false. We may imagine that Callistratus would have found himself in an awkward position, had Olympiodorus decided on suing him for the house rent; but we can hardly conclude that the possibility of such an event would constitute the basis of a right to impeach the evidence. The inference from the case is rather that anyone who wished, no matter what object he had in view, could prosecute a perjured witness. Naturally the instances of the exercise of such rights would be very few in comparison with the number of suits for perjury instituted by one or other of the parties.

No certain data are afforded by our authorities for determining whether a suit for perjury would lie in the case of evidence given before an arbitrator. Chrysippus v. Phormio seems to show conclusively that no action for perjury would be allowed, if the arbitration was a private one; for not only does the speaker state explicitly that there was no fear of punishment for giving false evidence before an arbitrator, but he complains that he was unable to reach his opponent's witness, who had committed perjury at the arbitration, but was not a witness at the subsequent trial.[2] Rentzsch's objection, that we cannot infer that this would apply to a public arbitration, has not as much weight as one would expect at first sight, since there was no appeal from a private arbitration, and the losing party would suffer more from false evidence than if the case was before a public arbitrator, whose decision was not final. But, apart from this, it is to be noted that the speaker is at no pains to state that he refers to a private arbitration; on the face of it, his language seems to apply to any arbitrator.[3] It is true that the jury might be supposed to be aware that he meant a private arbitration, as he had just explained that the parties to the suit had selected

[1] D. 48:44 ff.: οὐκ ἐπεσκηψάμην τοῖς μάρτυσι.

[2] D. 34:9, 46.

[3] D. 34:19.: πρὸς δὲ τῷ διαιτητῇ ἀκινδύνως καὶ ἀναισχύντως μαρτυροῦσιν ὅ τι ἂν βούλωνται.

the arbitrator. On the whole it is reasonably safe to conclude that false evidence before an arbitrator did not render a witness liable to an action for perjury.

It is incorrect, of course, to limit perjury to evidence given in court, for a false affidavit before the Archon in inheritance cases rendered the affiant liable to punishment.[1] As a party to a suit could himself make such a affidavit, it turns out that one who is in fact not generally a competent witness may still be prosecuted for perjury.[2] The claim of Apollodorus, however, that his opponent, Phormio, was liable to prosecution for perjury on the ground that he had virtually given evidence on his own behalf, because he was the real source of the alleged false evidence of Stephanus, need not be taken seriously.

Any kind of evidence, including an affidavit in support of a special plea,[3] hearsay evidence, and extrajudicial depositions,[3] could be attacked. It has been said[4] that a hearsay witness was liable to legal proceedings, if it could be proved that he had not in fact heard what he claimed he had heard; but it is impossible to imagine that such a situation could arise, as the mere admission by a witness that his evidence was hearsay would rule it out and render him liable, whether it was true or false.[5] If the extrajudicial deposition[6] was false, either the attesting witnesses or the original witness would be liable. The original witness would be liable, unless he could prove that he did not say in presence of the attesting witnesses what they claimed he said. There is no convincing proof that an oath in disclaimer (ἐξωμοσία) could ever be treated as false evidence. The technical word for false or perjured evidence is ψευδῆ μαρτυρεῖν or ψευδομαρτυρεῖν.[7] But in the passage cited to support the theory that an oath in disclaimer may be attacked as perjury only the word ἐπιορκεῖν is used, and evidently consciously used to avoid the technical words ψευδῆ μαρτυρεῖν. Æschines, when contemplating the possibility of a witness taking the oath of disclaimer, speaks of it as a shameless action, but says nothing of a prosecution, as he assuredly would have done had such an oath rendered the witness liable.[8]

The nature of the penalty attached to perjury has been the subject of some dispute.[9] It was regularly a fine, but the jurors had the right to

[1] D. 44:1 ff., 57 ff.

[2] M. S. L., p. 847.

[3] διαμαρτυρία, ἐκμαρτυρία.

[4] M. S. L., p. 879.

[5] D. 47:1.

[6] Cf. p. 25.

[7] D. *De F. L.*, 176; D. 45:58; William Wayte and C. R. Kennedy, *Dictionary of Antiquities*, *s. v.* μαρτυρία.

[8] Æsch. 1:47, 50.

[9] Rentzsch, p. 41 ff.; Thonissen, pp. 385 ff.; M. S. L., pp. 219, 486 ff.; Boeck, IV, pp. 120 ff.; Platner, I, 421.

inflict the loss of civic rights, if they chose.[1] Three convictions entailed a complete loss of civic rights. Regarding differences of opinion as to the part taken by the prosecutor in determining the penalty, it is sufficient to refer to the work of Rentzsch, where the whole matter is discussed. But it is so important to know whether the fine was paid to the prosecutor in the way of compensation, or to the public treasury in the way of a penalty, that it seems worth while to draw attention to several considerations which lead me to doubt that the fine was ever paid to the prosecutor in the way of damages. There is no direct statement in the Orators to this effect, nor is the language used ever inconsistent with a punitive fine.[2] Moreover, the almost unvarying use of the word ἁλίσκομαι, rather than of ὀφλισκάνω, in referring to the convicted witness, points to a purely criminal action. The form of pleading, too, which we have preserved in Apollodorus v. Stephanus,[3] does not contain the words ἔβλαψέν με, which might be expected in a suit where damages are sought.[4]

Apart from the question of language, several other circumstances should be noted. The gist of the offense is always said to be the deception practiced on the jury,[5] rather than the damage done to the prosecutor. The smallness of the penalty in case of failure is in the interest of the public rather than of the individual. Besides, several difficulties present themselves in the assessing of damages. What would be the measure of damages in cases arising out of criminal matters, where a stranger would be the plaintiff? Or how could damages be assessed at all until after the retrial of the main action, in cases where it could be reopened on proof of perjury? Or why should one prosecute singly several witnesses, if he could exact full damages from one?[6]

A witness to a writ of summons was liable, on proof of perjury, to a criminal prosecution[7] (γραφὴ ψευδοκλητείας). The penalty was at the discretion of the court, and was usually a fine for a first or second offense. For a third offense the punishment was loss of civic rights, which might be inflicted even for a first offense. A case occurs in which the jury proposed to inflict the death penalty; but there were several aggravating circumstances, including trespass, malicious destruction of property, and assault with intent. As all these offenses were proved in court, it is not strange that the jury was inclined to be severe.[8] Consequently, it cannot

[1] Platner, followed by Thonissen (*op. cit.*) believes that the loss was only partial, but there is no suggestion of this limitation in the Orators.

[2] D. 45:1; 47:2. [3] D. 45, 46. [4] Cf. D. 36:20. [5] D. 46:9; 47:1. [6] Isæ. 5:12.

[7] C. R. Kennedy, *Dict. Ant.*, *s. v.*; Thonissen, p. 390. [8] D. 53:15 ff.

be assumed that death was inflicted for the single offense of bearing false witness to a writ of summons.

Anyone who produced illegal evidence of any kind was liable, after the evidence had been impeached as perjured, to be sued for subornation of perjury (δίκη κακοτεχνιῶν).[1] As to the effect of a successful action for subornation of perjury and its relation to a retrial of the case (δίκη ἀνάδικος), there is no certain information in the authorities. Of four passages which deal with the conviction of a witness for perjury, two mention explicitly a δίκη κακοτεχνιῶν,[2] a third implies it,[3] while the fourth speaks of a retrial of the case.[4] In two other cases compromises were arranged as soon as it appeared that the witnesses were guilty of perjury.[5] The compromise in both cases had reference to the property in dispute, and not to damages that might have been collected from the witnesses or the party. The theory of Lipsius seems to fit the facts and the logic of the situation. He believes that the δίκη κακοτεχνιῶν was resorted to only when the person who was cast in the suit by false evidence had suffered a loss by the judgment and desired reparation from his opponent. To annul the judgment required a new trial,[6] which could be had without the intervention of an action for subornation as the result of a successful action against a witness for perjury in certain specified cases only.[7] To this explanation little can be added, except to suggest that, even if the unsuccessful suitor had suffered loss by the adverse judgment based on false evidence, he could scarcely succeed in an action for subornation, unless he could prove that his opponent was aware of the falsity of the evidence.[8] In other words, he would have to prove guilty knowledge of the character of the evidence, and not merely the introduction of false or illegal evidence. But, as a rule, it could be proved that the litigant was well aware that the evidence of his witness was false. If a party to a suit read an affidavit as that of a certain witness, without his knowledge or consent, he was liable to a suit for damages.[9]

1 D. 46:10. 2 D. 47:1; 49:56. 3 D. 46:10. 4 Isæ. 11:45.

5 Isæ. 5:13, 17. 6 M. S. L., pp. 977 ff. 7 Isæ. 11:45.

8 Platner (I. 416) notices this feature of an action for subornation of perjury, but is obliged to disregard it, because of his theory that it was a necessary step to securing a reversal of the original judgment.

9 D. 29:16.

INDEX OF GREEK LEGAL TERMS

INDEX OF PASSAGES CITED FROM THE ORATORS

PAGE

XXXIII

XXXIV

XXXV

XXXVI

XXXVII

XXXVIII

PAGE

XXXIX

XL

XLI

XLII

XLIII

PAGE

XLIV

XLV

XLVI

XLVII

XLVIII

XLIX

L

LII